MAYBE I SHOULD . . .

Case Studies on Ethics for Student Affairs Professionals

Edited by

**Florence A. Hamrick
Mimi Benjamin**

College Student
Educators International

University Press of America,® Inc.
Lanham · Boulder · New York · Toronto · Plymouth, UK

University Press of America,® Inc.
4501 Forbes Boulevard
Suite 200
Lanham, Maryland 20706
UPA Acquisitions Department (301) 459-3366

Estover Road
Plymouth PL6 7PY
United Kingdom

Library of Congress Control Number: 2009920163
ISBN: 978-0-7618-4546-1 (paperback : alk. paper)
eISBN: 978-0-7618-4547-8

Copublished by arrangement with the
American College Personnel Association

Dedication

To Greg Vitale and Rose A. "Posey" Kelly (my Gram)

ACPA Books and Media Editorial Board

Text Layout: Alexander K. Edwards, SEAC, LLC Toledo OH 43607

Table of Contents

viii

x

Preface

In writing and compiling the contents of this book, our overriding goal is to help new and midlevel student affairs professionals hone their ethical antennae for use in everyday situations with ethical dimensions. By focusing on situations faced by new professionals and midlevel administrators that are not and often will not become public, sensational, or lurid, individuals can become more skilled at discerning and responding to ethical considerations in situations that, at first glance, may not appear to have ethical dimensions or seem only mildly troubling. Specifically, this book is designed to help new and midlevel student affairs professionals heighten their knowledge of and sensitivities to professional ethics in practice, become aware of various ethical dimensions that tend to characterize student affairs work, identify and articulate plausible as well as preferred strategies for addressing ethically problematic situations, practice using formal statements on ethics and professional behaviors, and develop rationales to justify particular ethical decisions and actions. Advances in all of these areas foster a goal that we believe most of our colleagues share—that of becoming a more professional student affairs practitioner.

In light of our aims for this book, we provide readers with a brief overview of ethics and ethical decision making, strategies for analyzing ethical cases that incorporate working through sample cases, and opportunities to identify and analyze ethical considerations embedded in hypothetical situations that are commonly faced by new to midlevel student affairs professionals. Additionally, we offer resources and suggestions to instructors and facilitators who would like to incorporate ethical decision making and case studies into formal educational or staff development activities. Through use of these resources, readers can become increasingly sensitive to ethical dimensions within professional settings, participate effectively with colleagues in discussions of ethical considerations and warranted choices, and be better prepared to respond to ethical concerns that arise.

Although individuals representing a variety of backgrounds may find this book useful, it is clearly targeted to graduate students and entry-level to midlevel student affairs professionals. The book is appropriate for use as a text, a professional development resource, and a training resource for paraprofessional staff members. As we note in Chapter 1, the book—in particular, the collection of case studies—is best used in group settings with opportunities for shared exploration and discussion of the overt and inferred ethical dimensions, but solitary readers can certainly benefit from their individual analyses and reflections on the issues raised in the case studies.

The catalyst for this book was a course assignment in which second year master's level graduate students wrote short episodes that presented a realistic, ethically problematic situation in a setting relevant to new professionals in student affairs. Each student presented her or his episode and led an in-class discussion to surface the relevant ethical dimensions and develop warranted and defensible strategies to address the ethical problem(s). Some of these cases were quite realistic; most were adapted from the students' own experiences; and very few dealt with splashy, public episodes or situations where ethical lapses or transgressions were patently obvious. The assignment was intended to place professional ethics and ethical decision making in the foreground of students' attention, and the discussion aspect of the assignment required students to consult each other as well as relevant professional resources. The shared goal was to identify central considerations as well as ethically sound approaches to addressing or resolving the situation at hand. Ethical standards, principles, and guidelines that otherwise seemed to function at relatively abstract or simplistically applied levels were instead grounded in work situations with immediate relevance to new professionals. The discussions also highlighted the promise and power of group deliberations and consultations, particularly in cases where a complete range of ethically relevant dimensions were not immediately apparent—even to the author of a particular episode.

As instructors, we did not anticipate the generally high level of engagement in the assignment and the subsequent discussion. While we understood the benefits of soon-to-be new professionals as a group vetting interpretations and determining ethical, workable ways to address the situations at hand, the assignment apparently provided out-of-class fodder for continued discussion as well. A number of students reported that they engaged in continued discussion about the episodes with each other outside of class or continued their own ruminations about possible approaches should a similar situation present itself in their work. Despite the fact that the situations themselves were ones that would rarely attract media attention, or possibly because of this, graduate students readily envisioned themselves in similar situations as new professionals; most of the students were interested in acting ethically for reasons other than the potential risk of public exposure. We concluded that sharing and discussing such ethical episodes would provide low-risk but relevant practice in identifying ethical dimensions within everyday situations and engaging colleagues in solution-oriented discussions and deliberations. While these discussions might incorporate additional considerations related to case details, ethics and professionalism would be at the forefront of the discussions.

In our experiences, large-scale splashy situations with high probabilities of public exposure are often transformed into case studies, and such cases certainly provide important opportunities for professionals to engage in discernment, discussion, and potential resolution of the situations. As new professionals analyze such cases, they can prepare for how they might reason or act once they are in more senior administrative positions, and they can increase their appreciation of the complex situations and public scrutiny that accompany work as a senior student affairs administrator. However, the situations themselves may be less immediately relevant for new and midlevel student affairs professionals. The range of ethically problematic situations that most often confront new professionals—sometimes without notice—may inadvertently be minimized or dismissed because of the lower likelihood of exposure or public scrutiny, but we maintain that reflecting on situations that are comparatively low profile yet no less ethically charged can play a critical, targeted role in professional development. As an outgrowth of our prior case study experiences with graduate students, we concluded that a collection of everyday ethical case studies more relevant to entry-level to midlevel student affairs professionals would make a valuable contribution to literature on professional ethics, professionalism, and professional development in student affairs.

Moreover, we decided that the most promising authors of such cases would include graduate students and entry-level to midlevel student affairs professionals themselves. An open call for cases was launched in Fall 2004, and this announcement was forwarded to newsletters, networks, and professional association groups with disproportionate memberships of graduate students and new professionals. Many but not all of the case study authors who responded to this call were new to midlevel professionals.

To help us appraise the contributed cases, we convened a board of new to midlevel professionals to review the case submissions. We are grateful for the input and expertise from the following professionals who served as board members: Diann Burright, Kurt Earnest, Suzanne Harle, Ann Gansemer-Topf, Juan R. Guardia, R. Darrell Peterson, Heather Phillips, Leah Ewing Ross, and Bethany Schuttinga. The cases included in this book were selected following an anonymous review of each submission by at least two board members, and then, we as coeditors worked with each case study author where needed to revise or refine the cases that were selected for inclusion. After evaluating the strengths and relative balance of the accepted cases as a group, we invited additional authors to submit targeted cases to round out the case study collection. These invited cases were also blinded and reviewed by members of the board. This book represents the work and commitments of a large number of people, and we are thankful to the individuals who made contributions to this book at all levels.

Florence A. Hamrick, Ames, IA
Mimi Benjamin, Ithaca, NY
December 1, 2007

1

Overview

This chapter provides introductory information about ethics and ethical standards, professional identity development, and ethical decision-making in professional practice. However, it is well beyond the scope of this chapter to provide an exhaustive treatment of each of the topics above, particularly the broad topics of ethics and ethical decision-making. Numerous books and articles that focus more specifically on each of the above areas provide much more exhaustive treatments of the topics.

In this chapter, we instead summarize aspects that are relevant to the immediate purposes of working with ethical case studies as one form of professional development centering on ethics, ethical sensitivities, and ethical decision making. We provide a brief overview of ethics and professional ethics, discuss ethics as part of professional development and the formation of a professional identity, describe resources that are available as one contemplates and addresses ethically problematic situations, and describe processes for making ethically sound decisions and tracing one's rationales. In Chapter 2, specific strategies and approaches to analyzing ethical case studies will be presented along with the analysis of a sample case.

Attention to Ethics

Our guiding assumption in this chapter is that student affairs professionals should be actively and reflectively engaged in determining ethically sound choices and approaches to their work. Not only do ethical issues arise more frequently in practice than students in particular seem to believe that they will (Welfel, 1990), but being faced with ethical dilemmas is inevitable because the complexity of the world leads to contested claims about what is right and/or what should be done (Young, 2001). Not all ethically charged issues that arise for student affairs professionals are readily apparent, and very seldom do ethical problems announce their arrival with flashing strobes, beating drums, or exclamation points to provide convenient warnings.

Making a choice per se does not necessarily mean that one is facing a dilemma or an ethical dilemma. For example, a conflict between right and wrong is not a dilemma. Ethical dilemmas are dilemmas precisely because there are multiple plausible "right" answers, and making choices, setting policies, and reaching decisions can certainly present or raise ethical dilemmas. For example, June, a student government advisor, may support the student government's passage of a requirement that recognized student organizations submit twice-yearly audit reports (in August and February) in order to qualify for student activity fee allocations that are made each year by the student government. Such a policy is consistent with notions that most student affairs professionals would readily endorse, such as equal treatment of organizations, expectations of proactive officer responsiveness, and linking actions with consequences in support of learning.

However, June noticed that six months after the requirement went into effect (which included almost three months of summer vacation), approximately one-third of the student organizations, most of which had comparatively smaller memberships or had been founded only in the last few years, plus nearly all of the international student groups had not submitted their first required audit reports, making them technically ineligible to receive student activity fee funding for the following year. By contrast, almost all of the large, longstanding organizations had submitted their reports. After visiting with some of the affected organizations' officers, June became concerned about how and when organizations were notified of this policy change. The apparently uneven dissemination of information may have resulted in disparate or discriminatory impacts on organizations with smaller constituencies and members who tended to be less well-connected informally to student government members. At this point, June identified an ethical dilemma because equal treatment of organizations is right, but so is nondiscriminatory treatment of organizations.

To discern the ethical content of situations that constitute dilemmas, moral sensitivity, or comprehending the moral components of a situation, as well as a commitment to moral conduct are needed (Rest, 1986). Thoughtful engagement with the cases in this book can help advance professionals' moral sensitivity. Decisions about one's commitment to moral conduct, as well as follow-through on one's commitment, ultimately remain in the hands of individual professionals, like June as she considers whether and how to bring these concerns to the attention of student government officers.

What Are Professional Ethics?

Professionals are expected to act within appropriate ethical parameters and to employ professional ethics. But what are professional ethics? According to Winston and Saunders (1991),

> *"Ethics" from a philosophical point of view is concerned with determining what acts or behaviors are "right" or "ought to be done/not done," as well as determining the epistemological justifications for ethical statements or assertions. . . . "Ethics" is also used to describe the activity of specifying how and why some particular group of people decide a given behavior is right or wrong and then acts upon these decisions. (p. 311)*

In other words, the focus is not only on what perspectives or actions are "right," or "best," or "better," but also on the reasons that support the judgments and decisions that are made. Professionals who strive to conduct themselves ethically should focus not only on determining ethically sound responses to problematic situations but also on articulating and discussing the reasons that justify choosing these responses.

The terms "ethics" and "morals" often are used interchangeably by ethicists, because the words share a root that is similar in meaning (Nash, 2002). Conducting one's self morally similarly entails choosing ethically defensible perspectives and actions, as well as understanding and being able to communicate the rationales for choices: These are reasonable expectations for professionals. Professional ethics can be thought of as encompassing ends (the conclusions or actions) as well as procedures (the deliberative processes or criteria that guide ethical decision making). A wide range of resources, knowledge, and guidance can help student affairs professionals in their endeavors to make moral decisions and conduct themselves ethically. These resources include background beliefs, virtues, principles, and rules (Nash, 2002), which offer different, and sometimes conflicting, sources of information and grounds for determining what constitutes ethical conduct. As the following sections in this chapter suggest, becoming more aware of the range of ethical resources and deliberately tapping into each of these sources help professionals make better-informed ethical decisions and be better prepared members of their ethical community of colleagues (Canon, 1996). Before describing these sources of ethical information and knowledge, however, we discuss ethical decision making as a critical component of professionalism and fostering one's overall identity as a student affairs professional.

Ethics and the Development of a Professional Identity

Each day, in every student affairs setting, professionals are called on to make decisions and judgment calls at levels appropriate to their authority. Student affairs professionals in housing and residence life, for example, decide whether or not to contact health care or law enforcement professionals if threats to life or well-being are suspected. These same student affairs professionals also consult and collaborate with other professionals on campus to support students' ongoing academic and out-of-class success or to support a particular student's reentry to a campus residence following a disciplinary suspension.

Student affairs professionals are certainly concerned with particular students and particular settings, but a student affairs professional's work also happens within the larger contexts of institutional mission—with reference to specific policy and administrative frameworks, and within the still greater context of society at large. A given situation may happen on different campuses, and different professionals may well reach very different decisions. Both decisions can be right, correct, or appropriate. Family housing at one religiously affiliated institution may house families meeting certain definitions of family as set forth in institutional policies, while family housing at a public institution may be governed by policies that define eligible families quite differently. Decisions on granting housing contracts are justified by reference to formal policies and criteria as well as by reference to the respective housing professionals' interpretations of these policies and criteria in the context of institutional (and perhaps also departmental) mission. Being a professional presumes the exercise of mature judgment to help guide one's decision-making (Welfel, 1990), since policies and criteria are in practice applied to the real lives of people and in the context of sometimes deeply held institutional commitments and values.

Clearly, some basic guidance regarding what student affairs professionals "should" do can be secured by referring to policy manuals, handbooks, and other resources on procedures or processes. However, particularly when exceptional circumstances are at hand, when individuals request exemptions or waivers, or when professionals themselves question the rightness of certain policies or procedures, professionals also call on additional resources to guide their decisions or judgments on what should be done or what would be best to do given the specific circumstances. Indeed, professionals can consult, at formal or informal levels, a range of sources on ethics. Some sources, such as professional association statements regarding ethics or professional conduct (ACPA, 2006; National Association of Student Personnel Administrators, 1990), are formal, codified, and at times, prescriptive. Other sources of information are quite individualized and reflective, including the seasoning that is acquired from professional experience or the knowledge of institutional and departmental culture and values that can be gained from reflection or ongoing discussions with colleagues. Other referents, such as ethical principles or imperatives (e.g., Gilligan, 1993; Kohlberg & Hersh, 1977), can be seen as abstract and difficult to apply.

New professionals and midlevel professionals, who by definition have had limited opportunities for seasoning through long careers, nonetheless regularly face ethically problematic situations—particularly but not exclusively in their direct work with students. Ethically troubling situations can arise from something as simple as a quick, incautious, or unguarded response to a student's question that is taken as permission or an "okay" that was not intended, or situations can be as complex as protracted, formal decisions made in consultation with a supervisor or other colleagues over a long period of time. New and midlevel professionals are regularly in situations where they are expected to make ethically defensible decisions and represent a program or office in which students and colleagues can have confidence in its integrity. We do not argue that seasoning is sufficient proof of an ethically mature professional, only that longevity in the profession likely provides more experience dealing with ethical dilemmas. All professionals can benefit from developing heightened ethical sensitivities and systematic approaches to ethically problematic situations, and for new and midlevel professionals, this development can offset less experience in student affairs.

To varying degrees, graduate and professional education exposes individuals to information on professional ethics and related considerations. For example, Hoberman and Mailick noted that two expectations of professional education are "to socialize students in the 'thought processes' of the profession and to inculcate them with its customs, ethics, working relationships, and the behaviors expected from members of the profession" (1994, p. 4). Incorporating ethics into professional education is supported by relevant professional standards for graduate preparation programs in student affairs. The Council for the Advancement of Standards (CAS) stipulated that graduate faculty members inform students "of the ethical responsibilities and standards of the profession" (Council for the Advancement of Standards for Student Services/Development Programs, 1986, p. 108) as well as model ethical behavior and decision making in their work and their interactions with students. In addition, student development theory courses often include theories that describe development of moral reasoning, and practicum courses (and practicum experiences themselves) often include discussions of professional ethics in practice. Some graduate programs may infuse ethics across the curriculum or create additional strategies for educating graduate students about professional ethics.

However, exposure to information on ethics, moral reasoning, or professional ethics in practice through graduate education and associated experiences does not necessarily lead to stronger ethical awareness and practice as professionals. Incorporating ethics and ethical considerations into one's professional identity is more likely a process similar to incorporating other theoretical or relatively abstract material such as developmental, counseling, or administrative theories. Making these links to practice and grounding these considerations into one's professional values and commitments can be facilitated by providing new student affairs professionals with structured opportunities to reach their own interpretations of situations and decide what to do in response to what they identify as central, problematic aspects in situations. Such opportunities are provided through invitations to analyze current events that are unfolding on one's own or another campus; working through case studies with colleagues, supervisors, and/

or faculty members; or participating in ongoing reflective supervision meetings with advisors or site supervisors. Graduate programs can differ on the degree to which these structured opportunities are offered or emphasized due to curriculum requirements, credit hours, or other considerations. Consequently, even though new student affairs professionals often possess basic levels of information regarding ethical decision making and ethical standards, they may have experienced multiple or few opportunities for experiential or applied learning about ethics and conducting themselves ethically as professionals.

Additionally, for student affairs professionals who begin work in the field after earning a baccalaureate degree or after earning a graduate degree in another academic focus, their formal preparation related to professional ethics may well be minimal, or at least not targeted to ethics and ethical practice within student affairs. This book is offered as a supplemental resource to support the ongoing ethical development of student affairs professionals, and the book should also be useful for student affairs professionals with backgrounds, experiences, and formal education in other areas.

One promising entry into ethical awareness and ethical sensitivities for all professionals begins with regarding one's own thoughts and feelings as potential dissonance meters that can help identify ethically troubling situations and pinpoint the roots of potential ethical dilemmas. Rion's (1996) question, cited by Fried (2003, p. 116) "Why is this bothering me?" asks professionals to inquire into their reactions and invites professionals to ask whether they may have played a role in creating a now-troubling situation. This focusing question highlights the complex and personally grounded nature of ethical deliberations and of ethical situations as well and echoes our emphasis on the development of one's own professional identity as it is enacted within the contextual (e.g., individual campuses) nature of student affairs work. Rion's further question "Am I being true to myself?" also cited by Fried (2003, p. 117) highlights the importance of individual integrity to professional ethics. This question invites professionals to reexamine the status of one's own deeply held—yet also potentially maturing or evolving—commitments and the degrees of congruity between one's own commitments and the values, traditions, and expectations of one's employing institution or department. Case studies themselves can provide "instrument[s] of rich self-revelation" (Nash, 2002, p. 65) and thus can be central to one's continued professional development as individuals' guiding values and commitments are surfaced, revisited, or reinforced. As one's career and life progresses, and as one's department or institution evolves or changes, for example, under different leadership, the exercise of ethical reflection can help professionals trace the degree of professional fit or match and make informed decisions accordingly.

Finally, emphasizing the development of a professional identity with respect to ethics assumes that student affairs professionals themselves are human beings who are generally well intentioned but are also fallible and continue to grow. Rion's questions above invite professionals to explore their reactions as well as their own potential involvements in ethically troubling situations. Borrowing from feminist research and development of seasoned and alert researchers, Jagger recommended the recognition of what she called "outlaw" emotions, or a "'gut-level' awareness that [individuals] are in a situation of coercion, cruelty, injustice, or danger"(1989, p. 161) to ourselves or, perhaps more importantly, to others. Such recognition is important for professionals, because a common reaction to one's outlaw emotions is often self-isolation or suspicions of one's own incompetence, at the very time that one may need most to consult others and ask for help or advice with situations. Formal professional preparation regarding ethics can conceivably backfire if new professionals expect themselves to be fully prepared to face ethically troubling situations.

Sheryl Kleinman noted, "professional schooling often teaches students to present themselves as smart, thereby discouraging talk about their fears" (1991, p. 192). Not all graduate programs, or not all aspects of the graduate experience, may be perceived as comfortable places for sharing and discussing uncertainties, fears, or failings. If professionals have understanding faculty members, mentors, supervisors, and/or peers, they can continue to explore and utilize uneasy feelings productively without believing on some level that the new or relatively new status of "professional" allows for no mistakes or missteps while learning and continuing to develop as student affairs professionals. The use of hypothetical case studies such as those in this book provides a safety net of sorts for readers who will presumably suffer no work-related consequences for the interpretations and decisions made and instead can gain more information about themselves and about ethical dimensions and situations that are common within student affairs work.

If professional standards or formal statements were prescriptive and absolute sources of guidance in ethically problematic situations, no ethical decision making would be required of professionals—other than the choice to consult the appropriate statement and follow the relevant directive. But ethical situations in practice are contextualized in any number of ways, and professionals make ethical decisions in the absence of direct or unquestioned (or unquestionable) guidance. To echo Welfel (1990) above, professionals are professionals largely because they are trusted and relied on to make judgments, including ethical judgments. Making judgments and decisions is an inevitable part, and a rather large part, of being a student affairs professional. Knowing and being aware of multiple resources and information available on ethics and building more experience making ethical decisions will maximize the likelihood that one's professional identity will contain not only a strong commitment to ethics but also a commitment to becoming a more responsible, thoughtful, and reflective ethical decision maker.

While ethical dilemmas do not always have legal ramifications, it is important to note that some situations—including some case studies in this book—involve legal as well as ethical issues. Situations involving issues such as freedom of speech or due process are not uncommon in student affairs settings, and professionals must be familiar with not only ethical principles and guidelines but also judicial or conduct guidelines or procedures that are often institution specific. In a number of the case studies in this book, legal aspects should certainly be recognized and handled or referred appropriately as part of the case analysis, yet ethical considerations will often remain. Adherence to legal principles or code guidelines may not simultaneously remove or sufficiently address ethical dimensions. This caution would be particularly acute in situations where, for example, a code of conduct stipulation is in itself discriminatory or is selectively applied.

In the next sections of this chapter, we describe three sources of ethical information and perspectives available to professionals making ethical decisions. We do not argue that there are not more than three informational sources, but we feature these as perhaps the most encompassing relevant sources. We discuss the contributions as well as limitations of each and highlight the importance of consulting multiple sources and perspectives for ethical information rather than relying solely only one source.

Resources for Ethical Decision Making

Professionals, including student affairs professionals, have three major sources of information, knowledge, and perspective to help guide them in making ethical decisions and acting in ethically responsible manners. These are background beliefs, character or virtue, and principles. Nash (2002) refers to each as different moral "languages," which is consistent with his emphasis on professionals' abilities to articulate reasons for their decisions to choose one or more of these languages as appropriate to certain situations. These three sources are also referred to as "orientations" (Fried, 1997a), since each identifies a perspective from which situational interpretations and decision making proceeds. Identifying these as orientations for individuals, however, does not minimize the perceived importance of dialogue with respect to ethics and ethical decision making, which will be addressed in the section that follows this one.

Background Beliefs

According to Nash (2002), background beliefs include sources of moral authority in individuals' lives and histories that may be largely tacit and not easily accessible for articulation or examination. Nonetheless, the perspectives that they provide are central for understanding how individuals will tend to interpret situations and understand what would be right. Such beliefs can arise from, for example, groundings in religious traditions or practices, socialization, or prior experiences that now contribute to one's outlook on the world, supply one's moral reference points, and inform one's value systems. Because of the vast differences among individuals' experiences and background beliefs, Nash noted that individuals can face the same ethical dilemma yet not construct the ethical dilemma in the same way. One analogous example of such an interpretive difference that is familiar among student affairs professionals is Carol Gilligan's

(1993) use of literature on girls' socialization—primarily Nancy Chodorow's work—to help explain the care-oriented conceptions of ethics and contrast this perspective with the principled justice orientation found in Lawrence Kohlberg's work. The perspectives are not simply different in orientation, they operate to influence how individuals construct and interpret an ethical situation. Differences in constructions and perspective are crucial, with the Heinz dilemma as an example. In this situation, a man (Heinz) is unable to purchase a drug for his stricken wife from a pharmacist who insists on receiving full payment, and Heinz may consider stealing the drug to save his wife. This case can be regarded as a case of competing rights to life and to property; yet it can also be interpreted as a problem centering on cruelty, unreasonableness, and withholding of care that could be offered.

Nash (2002) further pointed out that many of these background influences operate on a largely unacknowledged level, which means that professionals may be unable to articulate their own critical background influences as a way to help communicate to others why they frame a situation or interpret the ethics involved in certain ways. For example, one student affairs staff member may enthusiastically support combining the traditional banquet for graduating seniors with an "etiquette dinner interlude" during which time a professional consultant will offer, using a portable microphone, his or her conclusions and advice regarding clothing, manners, posture, and associated social graces of the attendees. However, another staff member may be uneasy or nervous about the planned interlude but less well able to articulate reservations that are grounded, at least in part, in his own status as a first generation college student. He may be reminded on some level of life experiences that reinforced longstanding beliefs regarding formal social events, class status, and relative privilege among college students yet be less well able to articulate these beliefs and perspectives in this decision-making situation regarding potential negative impacts on first generation or similarly situated students who will be at this dinner, presumably to be honored. Graduate teaching, supervisory styles, and individual habits that emphasize reflection, acceptance of differences, and increased self-knowledge can help new and midlevel professionals consider the ways in which aspects of their individual backgrounds inform their perspectives, their working assumptions about the world, and what they value for themselves and others. This information, in turn, becomes a valuable source of ethically relevant perspectives and considerations that professionals will bring to bear on their work and on choices to be made.

Fried (1997a, 1997b) added that, given the growing presence of diverse students and staff members on campuses, student affairs professionals should not assume that their peers or students necessarily share similar backgrounds and influencing factors. Instead, professionals should expect that individuals perceive situations differently and reach different conclusions about the nature of ethical situations as well as preferable strategies or solutions. Far from constituting a weakness or fragmenting ethical considerations, these various backgrounds and cultural perspectives—and the values that are emphasized—serve to enrich and broaden the consequent ethical discussions and deliberations (Fried, 1997a, 2003).

Character or Virtue

The second moral language or moral orientation is character or virtue, which is grounded in one's experiences and identities in one's world(s). This orientation emphasizes the lessons learned through immersion in various communities, including one's educational and professional communities, and is commonly expressed as sets of virtues to be practiced and/or vices to be avoided (Nash, 2002). These sets of virtues and vices constitute in important ways the character of a person or the ideals to which she or he aspires that are consistent with the shared expectations of one's influential communities of reference. This perspective of ethics is also referred to as virtue ethics. Virtue ethics emphasizes the "characteristics of particular people in particular contexts. Virtues or traits are considered to be personal qualities that are deemed meritorious in a particular context" (Fried, 1997a, pp. 13-14). Attempts to articulate central moral virtues have included:

*Core human virtues of prudence, love, courage, love of God, justice, and hope (Meilaender, 1984, cited in Nash, 2002);

*Counseling psychologists' virtues (also adopted for student affairs professionals by Fried, 2003) of prudence, integrity, respectfulness, and benevolence (Meara, Schmidt, & Day, 1996).

Using this approach to ethics, when persons make a moral decision, they appraise, audit, and shape their own moral character (Nash, 2002), and their decision is an outward demonstration of this moral character. Acting consistently with one's ideals and virtues provides, upon reflection, input and further information about one's integrity of character as well as how one's character may be evolving or changing as a result of being part of new communities and having different sets of experiences.

The importance of professional communities like workplace settings or peer groups cannot be underestimated in virtue ethics, as Winston and Saunders (1991) emphasized:

> *A community, then, that deliberately and intentionally attends to ethical concerns every day provides the support that its members require to carry out the intellectually complex and personally challenging task of addressing the ethical quality of life. . . . Being part of a community that is committed to moral values increases the likelihood that we will act on ethical matters if they arise, and that we will do so with some consistency. (p. 74)*

The examples that professionals set with respect to acting ethically and exhibiting consistent virtues impacts individual professionals' growth and maturity, and virtuous examples contribute to the growth of others within the community and ultimately to the community's strength as a community of ethical reference. Informal and private conversations with peers and colleagues about troubling or difficult situations—often referred to as "shop talk"—allow professionals to engage in discussions about feelings, uncertainties, and ethical options with trusted persons. The foundations of one's ethical community can be established very early in one's career, for example, within a graduate school cohort or within a group of hall directors or admissions counselors. These trusted, valued colleagues can continue to listen and provide perspectives and feedback as ethically troubling situations arise throughout one's career.

As more formal communities, professional associations, and related bodies develop and codify ethical statements, rules, or guidelines that outline expectations of professionals in a particular specialty area, in many cases, central, guiding principles are incorporated within these statements to provide groundings or reference points for understanding the specific, more prescriptive or behavioral items.

Principles

The third moral language or perspective is one of principles. In student affairs literature, Kohlberg's justice (Kohlberg & Hersh, 1977) and Gilligan's care (1993) are common frameworks of ethical reasoning and ethics centered on conceptions of principles, injunctions, or imperatives. As with sets of moral virtues, sets of moral principles abound and, depending on the ethical frameworks, include principles such as fairness, maximizing benefits, universalization, and dignity/ respect (e.g., Robinson & Moulton, 1985). For example, the principle of fairness holds that "persons who are equal in aspects relevant to a particular situation should receive equal treatment" (Robinson & Moulton, 1985, p. 7), and the principle of dignity/respect both provides for the respectful treatment of others and prohibits exploitation.

The most familiar set of ethical principles among student affairs professionals is likely Kitchener's (1985) five ethical principles of benefiting others, or service to humanity; promoting justice, or ensuring fairness; respecting autonomy, or supporting freedom of choice; being faithful, or maintaining trust; and doing no harm, or avoiding injurious acts. These five principles appear in the "ACPA Statement of Ethical Principles and Standards" (2006) as "foundation for this document" (p. 10) and are more fully described in Appendix A of this book. The "CAS (Council for the Advancement of Standards in Higher Education) Statement of Shared Ethical Principles" (2006) is organized with reference to a group of seven principles—autonomy, nonmalfeasance, beneficence, justice, fidelity, veracity, and affiliation—that were identified through a systematic review of member associations' ethics statements or codes. Principles and the more specific guidance that results from them lead to a conception of professional ethics as agreed-upon standards or rules.

Professional Ethics and Professionalism

In fact, Winston and Saunders (1991) defined professional ethics as "a set of rules devised through a consensus of the profession that guides or specifies the parameters of the conduct of members of the profession when fulfilling professional responsibilities and roles" (p. 314). Although sets of rules—imperatives as well as prohibitions—can reflect professional ethics, particular virtues, beliefs, and values are also reflected in formal ethics statements. Since ethical statements represent deeply held values and commitments of a professional community (Winston & Saunders, 1991), they are intrinsically tied to the communities that created the statements. Furthermore, these professional communities revise their statements over time through dialogue about the shared values that should underpin the formal statements (Fried, 2003). For example, one analysis of the predominant values of the student affairs profession (Young, 2003) identified values that applied to individuals (wholeness, uniqueness, experience, responsibility) and contexts (community, equality, justice) and positioned caring as both an instrumental value of practitioners as well as a goal of student affairs practice (pp. 98–101).

In the student affairs profession, ethical standards have been published by two national umbrella organizations (NASPA, ACPA) and numerous associations of professionals employed in various specialized areas. More recently, a "Statement of Shared Ethical Principles for CAS Member Organizations" (2006) has also been codified, even though ethical guidance and directives for a range of student affairs areas have regularly appeared within earlier versions of CAS Standards. Although many of the topics addressed are similar within the NASPA and ACPA statements, one principle orientation differs. The NASPA statement tends to place primary emphasis on members' responsibilities to their employing institutions, while the ACPA statement tends to disproportionately emphasize members' responsibilities to students and to their professional duties (Canon, 1996; Fried, 2003). These orientations have remained consistent through the most recent round of revisions (ACPA: College Student Educators International, 2006; National Association of Student Personnel Administrators, 1990). Individuals who are members of professional organizations are expected to understand and adopt the ethical standards of that association (or those associations), even though enforcement and sanctioning mechanisms for alleged violations are relatively weak in comparison to other professional associations such as the American Psychological Association (Welfel, 1990).

The norms of a campus community, as well as the perhaps different norms of the surrounding community, bring to bear additional sets of values that influence professionals' interpretations of ethical principles and standards and, in turn, their ethical decision making (Fried, 2003). When starting a new job or moving to a different campus, it may take a good deal of time to understand the values and culture of a campus and the surrounding community(-ies). Although professionals are responsible for learning and understanding these features, supervisors (and supervisors of graduate interns) also share the responsibility for helping professionals in these areas (Janosik, Creamer, Hirt, Winston, Saunders, & Cooper, 2003). In particular, supervisors should be explicit about how institutional, division, and program values inform expectations, and they should help staff members differentiate between espoused and actual values. Also, in the case of internships, supervisors should allow interns to opt out of the assignment if the fit is poor or if particular needs of the site, such as expectations of work on one's Sabbath or during one's times of prayer, are at odds with the intern's religious practices or values or cultural commitments. New and midlevel professionals should not be left to figure these out by trial and error alone, making mistakes in the process (Janosik et al.), but new staff members may need to initiate these explorations, ask questions, and engage colleagues in conversation about prevailing workplace values and norms. This information provides valuable local context for the more general ethical principles or imperatives as well as for the codified ethical standards and statements on professional ethics.

New professionals, midlevel professionals, and professionals new to student affairs should spend time clarifying and analyzing their background beliefs and their understandings of virtues and character. These understandings, along with greater familiarity with statements on professional ethics, provide the groundwork for the development of one's professional identity and enable one to take productive part in conversations with colleagues about ethical matters or troubling situations. However, depending solely on moral virtues, background beliefs, or ethical principles and standards to provide ethical guidance is insufficient grounding for professionals, who should instead utilize available ethical resources in combination.

Ethical Resources in Combination

Ethical decisions are impacted by such factors as religious beliefs, previous education, personal values, and the ethical behaviors of mentors or others (Winston & Saunders, 1991, p. 324). Ethical codes, and even laws, may have less of an impact on decision making than generally accepted ethical principles like preventing harm and benefiting others. However, challenges to ethical decision making occur "when principles, values, or institutional needs are in conflict, as they frequently are" (Winston & Saunders, 1991, p. 324).

Although three orientations to ethics were outlined above, each individual orientation represents an incomplete framework for higher education professionals who work in an increasingly heterogeneous and multicultural society (Fried, 1997b):

> [A]ll postsecondary education in the United States involves students, administrators, and faculty members from many cultures. . . . [E]thical practice must consider the presence of different cultural perspectives on campus and use these perspectives to educational advantage whenever possible. The ethical system that dominates higher education in the United States then becomes one

*of many to be considered in decision-making, ethical relationship, and ethics
education, rather than the only valid point of view or the dominant perspective.
(p.1)*

Because members of various groups have different needs and expectations,
ignoring or not attending to "this vast range of expectations and priorities is to
violate both ethical principles and virtues" (Fried, 1997a, p. 19).

Ultimately, myriad perspectives and sources of personal, professional, and
institutional information constitute ethical resources for professionals. In ethical
decision-making, not only facts but values impact the process, since "the values
placed on facts, which form the basis for moral judgments, are subjective, or
dependent on the individual viewpoint" (Robinson & Moulton, 1985, p. 9).
We would add that shared cultural values also influence how facts, events, or
actions are regarded and valued. With respect to institutional values, May (1990)
cautioned that accessing these values is normally not easy: "Most of the mores
of the academy exist in unwritten form. . . . [I]t is important for an institution to
define its values and guidelines clearly and to communicate them to everyone
within the institution" (p. 17). Mission statements and vision statements can
provide information regarding espoused values and commitments, yet length of
tenure at an institution along with more experiences of local ethical dilemmas and
their resolutions can foster even greater knowledge of institutional values as they
are enacted.

Practicing ethical decision making, either through case analyses or actual
situations, provides professionals with further, experiential understandings of
relevant guidelines and principles, and these deeper understandings can foster
greater familiarity with ethical sensitivities and considerations that can be reflected
in professionals' everyday work. In terms of ongoing professional development,
addressing situations or cases and then reflecting upon one's assumptions and
courses of action yields greater self-knowledge and insight into one's own values,
evolving viewpoints, and perceived congruence with institutional culture. All of
this knowledge impacts the kind of professional that one is and that one seeks to
become.

Cultivating Ethical Behaviors and Habits

Ethical behavior, according to Canon (1996), can be fostered in three ways.
First, members of a professional organization can abide by relevant and agreed-
upon standards and expectations for professionals. Second, professionals can use
ethical principles to address ethical dilemmas they encounter in their practice.
Third, ethical behavior can be fostered by the expectations and values of one's
environment, including one's work setting. However, these approaches can and
do conflict at times (Canon, 1996), such as when a professional's decision, while
consistent with ethical principles, does not conform to the predominant values
held by one's immediate colleagues or supervisor. For example, a professional
may honor a student's autonomy by helping her or him learn about and secure

birth control devices, but a university that adheres to a different set of values and commitments regarding sex will not regard the professional's choice or behavior to be ethical. Canon (1996) identified additional considerations for ethical conduct in student services:

Key issues include (1) being able to recognize ethical dilemmas as such when they arise, (2) having a set of usable principles to guide our response to those dilemmas, (3) having a professional ethical code that addresses such matters, (4) knowing if and how to intervene, (5) determining how to respond to coworkers who may play a role in the evolution of an ethical dilemma, and finally, (6) actively fostering an environment that supports and promotes continuing inquiry into ethical matters. (pp. 106-107)

Professionals must consider individual beliefs, values, and cultural heritage; knowledge of ethical imperatives and principles; expectations for professionals as outlined in professional standard and ethical statements; and knowledge of our institutional and campus contexts. With this multifaceted knowledge, professionals become more sharply attuned to ethical dimensions of everyday situations and their roles and responsibilities for making ethical decisions. Through dialogue with others, professionals come to better understand their own evolving positions and gain insights into alternative interpretations that can enrich their appreciations of the complexities of ethical situations. Finally, by engaging candidly and honestly in conversations with trusted colleagues about ethical uncertainties or troubling situations, professionals become better equipped to participate in the ongoing discussions on our campuses, among colleagues, with students, and within the student affairs profession about what is right, wrong, better, worse, appropriate, or irresponsible.

Indeed, characteristics that support "good moral conversation" (Nash, 2002, p. 25) include habits of open-mindedness, listening intently, challenging respectfully, and making efforts to interpret situations and understand them. In the following chapter, we focus on strategies that emphasize this careful and deliberate approach to ethical case studies. In Appendix C, we offer instructors and facilitators suggestions to help foster a respectful and open environment that can be home to frank and potentially self-cautious or awkward discussion of ethics and ethical choices.

Student affairs professionals are expected to conduct themselves and their work in light of ethical considerations. The process of making ethically defensible and warranted decisions is contextualized by self, values, principles, standards, colleagues, and institutional setting. No single way of addressing any given ethical situation is the only way, and no approach or strategy is itself either complete or problem-free. According to Nash (2002), decisions are always accompanied by "moral traces" (p. 167), or doubts and cautions that can linger and themselves foster further reflection and learning. However, utilization of all available ethical resources and persons can yield more confident, defensible approaches to addressing ethically problematic situations. The following chapter provides one example of a systematic approach that can be applied to case study analysis and can also be adapted for reflective use in actual situations.

2

Analyzing
the Case Studies

Case studies can be a reflective professional development approach (Janosik et al., 2003) where staff members examine realistic situations, problem solve, and reflect on their learning. Case studies also provide an opportunity for the kind of role taking that engages persons with their environment (including peers) and encourages the temporary adoption of different viewpoints that can enlarge one's own perspectives (Kohlberg & Hersh, 1977).

This chapter provides strategies and suggested methods for approaching and analyzing systematically the cases in the subsequent sections of the book. Although some of the recommended steps may appear to be quite obvious (e.g., "Who are the main characters in the situation?"), answering other questions may generate information or plausible inferences that were not apparent from a first reading of the case (e.g., "Who is engaged in or affected by the situation?") and may reveal greater complexities within the case. A systematic approach to reading and closely analyzing the case studies will help uncover possible lurking dimensions for which ethical considerations may not have been immediately apparent.

We do not suggest that the approach outlined in this chapter is the only way to approach the cases, but the approach will provide an initial framework that can be customized or tailored. This framework, plus individual tailoring, can ultimately inform how professionals analyze and address ethically relevant situations in their own lives and work. All of the cases in this book are hypothetical—although many are adapted from real-life occurrences—so experimenting with one's own variations to the approach suggested in this chapter may help illuminate different aspects of the situations and help develop one's own repertoire of skills and approaches in potentially troubling situations.

A number of authors have provided guidance about processes to employ and which content is important to consider in ethically relevant situations. For example, resolutions to ethical dilemmas should consider "the act, the intention, the circumstance, the principles, the beliefs, the outcomes, the virtues, the narrative, the community, and the political structures" (Nash, 1996, p. 20). Canon (1989) suggested that practical matters be addressed, such as distinguishing legality versus ethicality and recommended using a trusted colleague for consultation when ethical dilemmas emerge. Canon also recommended that, in cases of suspected ethics violations, resolution should be sought with targeted individuals first, and that these contacts be made in a caring fashion. Finally, he suggested seeking both formal and informal reactions from colleagues and students regarding potential ethical implications, including additional ethical implications to which the situation may give rise.

The framework provided below emphasizes a careful reading of each situation followed by identification and then examination of concerns or problems. These concerns and problems are then cast in terms of relevant ethical principles, virtues, and/or professional standards. People (or in terms of these case studies, "characters") and their respective positions, opinions, and involvements are also critical elements to understand in each situation. In the final analysis, readers are asked to identify warranted strategies for action that can or should be taken by the central character in the case study, but these recommendations are not the final task. The final task is for professionals to explain the rationales that underlie their recommended strategies and decide how and to whom these rationales should be communicated if one is acting ethically.

Framework for Case Analysis
The steps identified below form a recommended approach to reading and analyzing the case studies. If a group is engaged in analyzing a single case, the group members together should determine when and how to discuss input and various perspectives on the issues. It may be fruitful for group members to answer the specific items under each header independently before sharing their findings with other group members so that the range of considered perspectives are captured and all members' input can be considered by the group. We recommend that readers make notes so that their perspectives, opinions, and interpretations are not lost during subsequent periods of group discussion.

Identify Relevant Situational Characteristics
- Who are the main characters in the situation?
- Who are the supporting or peripheral characters?

• What are the reporting, advising, or other work relationships relevant to the situation?

• What kind of institution, program area(s), and work settings are specified, and in what ways are these relevant to the situation?

• What are the temporal characteristics involved (e.g., time of semester, relative experience level(s), requests for meetings or other contact), and in what ways are these relevant to the situation?

Analyze the Situation

• What is troubling, disturbing, or of concern to you in the case? Identify and describe the problematic aspect(s) as you see it (or them).

• What makes certain aspects of this situation troubling, or a concern for you? Consult your own background beliefs and core values.

• Are there aspects in this situation that, while perhaps not troubling to you, might be troubling to others involved in this situation or impacted by it?

• Who is engaged in and/or affected by the situation?

Consult Ethical Principles

• Act to benefit others: In what ways are people benefited, disadvantaged, disserved?

• Promote justice: In what ways is the cause of justice advanced, promoted, stymied, or threatened?

• Respect autonomy: In what ways is autonomy protected, advanced, violated, or curtailed?

• Be faithful: In what ways is faith or trustworthiness present, absent, or compromised?

• Do no harm: In what ways are individuals' well being, worth, or dignity advanced, threatened, or ignored? (Kitchener, 1985; also referenced in ACPA and NASPA documents in Appendix A)

Identify and Consult Relevant Ethical Standards

• Which of the specific ethical standards or provisions from the ACPA, NASPA, or CAS statements (see Appendix A) provide guidance for understanding and addressing this situation? Do ethical standards or provisions from other groups such as specialty associations apply, and if so, which groups and which standards?

• In what ways do the relevant standards or principles reinforce each other as applied to this situation? In what ways are the relevant standards or principles inconsistent, and how do you reconcile any conflicts among them?

Identify the Decision Makers

• Who, if anyone, should make decision(s) and/or take action(s) in the short term? In the long term?

- Who should be consulted about this situation and potential short-term decisions or actions? Long-term decisions or actions?
- Who, if anyone else, should also be called upon to make decision(s) and/or take action(s) about contextual situations or concerns (e.g., policy considerations, contributing or aggravating factors)?

Recommended Actions and Strategies
- What actions should be taken?
- What are your rationales for recommending that these actions be taken?
- What actions, while perhaps tempting, should not be taken?
- What is your rationale for cautioning against taking those actions?

Appraise the Decision
- Revisit the five ethical principles above to evaluate your recommended decisions and actions. In what ways do your decisions and actions serve to benefit others, promote justice, respect autonomy, demonstrate faithfulness, and do no harm?
- What, if any, changes would you suggest for the characters or case settings that could minimize the likelihood of a future, similar occurrence?

Contextual Factors
- Suggest hypothetical changes to the events, circumstances, or characters, and brainstorm how these alterations may impact you analyses and ethical decision making. Such changes can amplify certain aspects or raise additional issues in the cases, ultimately reinforcing the contextual sensitivities of perceptions and ethical judgments.

Case Study and Analysis
Next, we present a sample case study and utilize the framework above to guide our analyses and structure our decision making and recommendations. First, read the following case study carefully and completely. Make notes of key facts as well as your initial interpretations and reactions.

Intimate Matters by Juan R. Guardia

> Eucalyptus College (EC) is a public Hispanic Serving Institution (HSI) enrolling 10,000 undergraduate and 1,200 graduate students. EC is located in a midsized city in the southeastern United States. Most EC students are from the home state and 39% identify as Latino/a, but many students are attracted from out-of-state to study the life sciences. EC is nationally known for its ecology programs, and it benefits from its relative proximity to inland ecosystems as well as the Atlantic and Gulf coasts. The EC student population is predominately nontraditional, with an average undergraduate student age of 29.

In addition to a small collection of science graduate programs, mostly at the master's degree level, EC also has had a two-year (full-time) master's degree program in higher education and student affairs since the late 1970s. A number of prominent student affairs professionals in the state graduated from the program, and this reputation attracted Luisa, 27 years old, and Joe, 29 years old, who are both first year students in the master's program. Luisa worked in a variety of positions at a nearby college before starting the higher education program, including admissions and residence life, but she decided that it was time to work toward the master's degree so she would be qualified for higher level positions in student affairs. EC is the first HSI Luisa has attended, and she enjoys the mix of students, many of whom share her Cuban heritage. Joe recently completed his undergraduate degree in biology at EC and enrolled in the program after having valuable opportunities as a student leader during his undergraduate experiences. A student of Irish and English heritage from the northeastern United States, Joe also enjoys the multicultural environment of EC and plans to stay in the area after he graduates.

Luisa and Joe are both graduate assistants (GAs) for EC's Office of Student Activities and Leadership (OSAL). Joe's responsibilities include advising clubs and organizations and the homecoming chairs. Luisa works primarily with the student programming board and union activities, although she and Joe have had to address Joe's ongoing frustrations that many Latino/a officers of various student clubs continue to approach Luisa first for advice on EC policies and for informal chats. Their supervisor is Mark Smith, the OSAL Director, who is new to his position this year. Mark is a recent graduate of a higher education master's program in the Midwest, where he served as a graduate assistant in the student union. Mark is 24 years old and White.

Joe and Luisa get along well as colleagues and enjoy each other's company. Both have recently expressed to Mark their intentions to return to OSAL as GAs the following academic year. The Tuesday before spring break, Luisa invited Joe to dinner at her apartment. During dinner, Luisa and Joe discuss their strong attractions to each other that have been growing since the beginning of the previous fall. They begin to kiss, and ultimately, they have sex. The following day, Joe and Luisa made the decision to pursue their intimate relationship, because it is consensual and because no one has mentioned any policies at EC that restrict such relationships. Within a week's time, Joe and Luisa became open about their relationship among their friends and fellow graduate students, although neither has discussed the relationship with Mark, who recently returned from his trip to a national student affairs meeting. Whispered conversations about the relationship began to emerge in the student affairs division offices. The dean's administrative assistant, Julia, called Mark to request that he meet with the Dean of Students the following day. After they agree on a time, Mark asks what the meeting will be about. Julia replies, "He wants to know what's going on with your two GAs and what you plan to do about it."

What should Mark do and why?

We will now proceed with analyzing the above case by addressing the questions and steps outlined in the approach above. Addressing these questions yields a more detailed reading of the situation and helps identify knowledge gaps as well as additional points to consider.

Identification of Relevant Situational Characteristics

Joe, Luisa, and Mark are the main characters in the situation. The dean is becoming a main character due to his initiation of a meeting with Mark, and the dean (via Julia) is the catalyst for Mark's new awareness that "something" is happening that involves his two graduate assistants. Supporting characters in the situation include Joe and Luisa's fellow graduate students who have been made aware of the relationship and who have helped spread the word. Other supporting or peripheral characters include student affairs staff members and students with whom Joe and Luisa work, since their curiosities may be piqued not only about the relationship per se but also about how work relationships and intimate relationships are condoned or regarded at EC. In terms of reporting lines, Joe and Luisa clearly report to Mark, and it is implied that Mark reports directly or indirectly to the Dean of Students. Joe and Luisa are colleagues to their fellow graduate students in the program and to persons in the student affairs division. Joe and Luisa both work with students, including student leaders, through their work at OSAL, although Latino/a students often approach Luisa instead of Joe, which is of concern to Joe, at least. Additionally, since Joe just graduated from EC the year prior and was a student leader as an undergraduate, some of his advising relationships may be with students for whom he was recently a peer.

EC is a public institution, which is relevant for a number of reasons. Extramarital sexual activity may be frowned upon at any institution, but if EC were private and/or religiously affiliated, this activity could constitute grounds for dismissal of a student or the termination of a staff member. As graduate students, Joe and Luisa could be considered students, staff members, or both by EC. It is unclear from the case study whether EC has personnel policies that prohibit or accommodate (e.g., in terms of administrative arrangements) intimate relationships among employees; if so, Joe and Luisa are not aware of such policies. The case makes no mention of Joe and/or Luisa being married or in committed partnerships with other people, so we assume that each is single. Either of them being in a committed relationship may lead to different interpretations of their intimate relationship by colleagues at either a public or private institution, and these interpretations can impact perceptions of professionalism or effectiveness. It is clear from the case that, while Joe and Luisa shared the news of their relationship among friends and colleagues, they had not informed Mark, their supervisor.

Joe and Luisa are well into the second semester of their first year in the master's program, and both have expressed their interest in returning to OSAL as GAs during their second year in the program. It is unclear whether Joe and Luisa are the sole GAs in OSAL or if there are additional GA staff members in this office or closely related units. Although Mark is the full-time OSAL professional as well as the supervisor in this situation, he is also younger than both Joe and Luisa. Among the three main characters, it appears that Luisa may have the most full-time experience in student affairs, since she gained a number of years of work experience before entering the master's degree program.

There is no information about the quality of work relationships between Mark and Joe or Mark and Luisa, and no indications about the quality of overall job performance of any of the three individuals. Alternately, there is no information to indicate that work relationships are not strong or that work performance all around has been unsatisfactory. Mark has apparently made no decisions regarding next year's GA staffing for OSAL, and it is unclear whether Mark is aware of the concerns surrounding students' contacting Luisa about issues for which Joe is responsible. While Luisa and Joe are finishing up their first year as graduate students, Mark is finishing up his first year at EC and completing an initial cycle at EC—learning more about the institution and aspects of culture, traditions, and expectations. Unless Mark attempts to postpone his meeting with the dean the next day (and is successful at doing so), he has a limited amount of time to prepare for this meeting. No information in the case study characterizes the prior relationship between Mark and the dean. We know very little about the dean except that he has requested a meeting for the purposes that Julia communicated to Mark.

Situational Analysis

Different people may initially be troubled, or less troubled, by some aspects of the case than others, and some people may determine that nothing is troubling. Individuals' standpoints and interpretations can often provide insights into background beliefs, worldviews, and commitments to certain values and principles. We will discuss a number of aspects of the case that may raise concern and acknowledge that there may be other aspects as well.

First, it may be troubling to some readers that Joe and Luisa have engaged in intimate relations outside of marriage because of commitments to values that may be grounded in a variety of religious or cultural beliefs that makes such relations problematic or objectionable. Additionally, issues of fairness may influence one's reaction to an intimate relationship between two coworkers, since concerns can arise about partisanship and extra loyalties between colleagues who are also intimate partners. Particularly if Joe and Luisa work with one or two fellow GAs in OSAL or a closely related unit, their GA colleagues may wonder whether Joe's and Luisa's intimate relationship may entail special work-related considerations for each other that would not be extended to the other GAs or other staff members with whom they work. A similar concern could arise among fellow graduate students with respect to group projects or course assignments.

It may be troubling to some individuals that Joe and Luisa did not inform their supervisor about their personal relationship. As potential complications, it appears that Mark had only recently returned to campus and that many of these events transpired around and during spring break. Joe and Luisa may have assumed that Mark would hear about their relationship through the local grapevine that was activated when they told their fellow students, and additionally, that this is an appropriate method for their supervisor to learn of their relationship. They may also have thought that it was an awkward subject to raise with a supervisor or that their relationship should not be Mark's concern. Readers may conclude that Joe and Luisa's actions run counter to values of openness and respect that are conveyed by communicating information directly. Other readers may determine that, if one proceeds from primary commitments to privacy and respect for individuals' personal lives, very little is troubling about this situation, since a consensual intimate relationship is personal business that need not be shared with others at all.

Other issues or concerns may extend to Mark and to the dean. Mark has been asked to discuss information relating to his staff members of which he is currently unaware. Mark's lack of awareness can call into question for some, and perhaps for the dean in this case, Mark's effectiveness as a supervisor as well as his staff members' regard for him as their supervisor. These concerns could be grounded in factors such as the relative age differences between Joe and Luisa and their younger supervisor Mark and Mark's evolving professional reputation at EC. A number of people are directly or indirectly impacted by the situation, including graduate students and other staff members or students who may harbor curiosities about consensual relationships and if and how such relationships are received at EC. Additionally, EC students and, in particular, students involved in OSAL programs may reach very different conclusions on the relevance of Joe's and Luisa's personal relationship to their working relationships and work effectiveness.

Ethical Principles

Although Mark should respect the autonomy of Joe's and Luisa's decision to pursue a relationship, EC personnel policies may curtail the full exercise of Joe's and Luisa's autonomy, and if so, Mark as their supervisor may play a central limiting role. Mark should respond faithfully to the dean's request by making every effort to provide factual and complete information. However, Mark should also strive through his exercise of confidentiality and discretion to prevent or minimize harm to Joe and Luisa that ongoing campus gossip or curiosity can foster. In terms of fairness, Mark should strive to be fair to Joe and Luisa as he considers his OSAL staffing decisions. Additionally, Mark should also consider the standing of his other staff members who may fear being disadvantaged at work by Joe's and Luisa's extra measure of loyalty or dedication to each other or, alternately, by work-related impacts related to personal relationship difficulties among colleagues or Joe's and Luisa's potential breakup.

Ethical Standards and Considerations

Each of the three ethical statements provides insight and guidance to help Mark identify ethical dimensions of this situation and determine an initial response. Many of the formal standards echo the principles and considerations outlined above. For example, professionals are obligated to inform supervisors and other appropriate persons of situations that may be disruptive or may impinge on effectiveness (e.g., ACPA 3.5, 3.6; NASPA 3) while also respecting individuals' decisions, treating individuals with dignity and fairness, and extending appropriate confidentiality (e.g., ACPA 3.7; NASPA 7; CAS Autonomy [2,3,6], Justice [1,4,5], Fidelity [1,2], Veracity [1,2,3]). Professionals act in accordance with their institution's mission or policies (e.g., ACPA 3.1; NASPA 1, 2; CAS Justice [5], Fidelity [4]), being sensitive to the particular character of the institutions and communities where they work and live (e.g., ACPA 4.4; NASPA 6; CAS Fidelity [4]). However, professionals may also choose to initiate discussions of questionable policies, practices, or conventions based in reasons of, for example, professional ethics, social justice, or individual conscience. Professionals also understand the potential employment-related consequences of their objections and/or actions (e.g., ACPA 3.2, 3.19, 4.4, Context: Culture; NASPA 5).

On a fundamental level, the statements indicate that professionals have a responsibility to address concerns and perceived problems (e.g., ACPA 3.2, 3.10; CAS Beneficence [3]), seeking guidance or assistance where needed (e.g., ACPA 1.4). Professionals are also responsible for participating in the continuing professional development of supervisees—including students—and this responsibility incorporates attention to ethical issues and standards (e.g., ACPA 1.2, 2.11, 2.16; NASPA 17). Finally, supervisors should be involved in defining responsibilities, expectations, and evaluation criteria for the staff members they supervise (ACPA, 3.10, 3.11), recognizing that these elements may evolve over time or in response to specific situations.

A number of central initial considerations are reinforced by the above standards, including sharing of relevant information between Joe and Luisa with Mark, and Mark with the dean. Any of these parties may reach a different determination of what is relevant to share and with whom, and respectful discussions should then occur to reach a shared understanding of what is work related, what is personal, and how these may overlap. If reaching a shared understanding is not possible, respectful articulations of the issues underlying one's subsequent positions are warranted. As a supervisor, Mark should discuss with Joe and Luisa relevant professional and ethical implications of their personal decisions and the potential resulting implications for his decisions regarding their work. As a supervisee, Mark is also responsible for discussing with his supervisor relevant aspects of the situation and Mark's thoughts, decisions, and recommendations. As he makes decisions and engages in these discussions, Mark should follow any applicable institutional policies or procedures and conduct himself with respect, circumspection, prudence, and integrity.

Identification of Decision Makers

The dean, through Julia, has identified Mark as a decision maker already by his request to hear from Mark "what you plan to do about it," suggesting that the dean considers the situation at least somewhat problematic. The dean may well help determine the final decisions, but according to the case, he first wants to hear information and potential solutions from Mark, the immediate supervisor. Joe and Luisa will also decide, at the least, what they will disclose to Mark about their relationship and how they are managing (and should manage) their work relationship in light of their new personal relationship. Mark, however, will determine (perhaps in conjunction with the dean) to what extent the work relationship at OSAL will continue and what, if any, conditions should be stipulated to ensure continued OSAL effectiveness and functioning. Consequently, Joe and Luisa separately or together will determine their levels of compliance with any such stipulations and weigh the professional consequences of noncompliance. Depending on the relationship between assistantship sites and the graduate program as well as local conventions, the department head or the students' faculty advisors may be informed or consulted regarding the situation and assistantship staffing decisions and/or conditions. If EC has policies regarding consensual relationships between coworkers, the human resources office may have a consulting or decision-making role in determining accommodations or appropriate arrangements. Alternately, this decision making may be reserved on a case-by-case basis for the immediate supervisor or the supervisor of the department or division. In the solutions recommended below, we will consider a sampling of these hypothetical possibilities.

Recommended Actions and Strategies

Mark may wish to try to postpone the meeting with the dean until he gathers information and has had a chance to speak with Joe and Luisa and consult any relevant policies. This decision may largely depend on Mark's relationship with the dean and understanding of work style. If the meeting goes forward before Mark can gather necessary information, Mark should honestly convey his lack of complete information thus far but may initiate a discussion with the dean regarding his planned processes for collecting information and the potential decisions that will be made, such as on contract renewals. The dean has an opportunity to weigh in if he wishes, and Mark has conveyed honestly what he can at this point and outlined his follow-up process.

If Mark discovers that EC has policies regarding consensual employee relationships, he should follow this policy closely as he works with Joe and Luisa and the dean. If anyone, including Mark, finds problems or concerns about the policy as written or as implemented in this situation, institutional channels should be used to express these concerns and seek a hearing, an exception, or revision, depending on the preferred outcome. If EC does not have policies regarding consensual relationships, Mark should create an arrangement that will suffice for the remainder of the year—and into next year if Mark decides to renew their GA contracts. It is generally unacceptable for Mark or the dean to require that Joe and Luisa terminate their intimate relationship, but the particular social and moral character of the institution or the community may also greatly impact Joe's, Luisa's, or both of their subsequent effectiveness as student services staff members at EC. In this situation, Mark may well decide or be pressed to take a more immediate work-related action, such as immediately terminating or reassigning Joe, Luisa, or both for the remainder of the current contract period. If Mark decides to accommodate the relationship between his OSAL staff members (at minimum, for the remainder of the year), the terms of the arrangement should focus on work-related effectiveness and fairness, such as ensuring that Joe and Luisa do not report to each other on projects or that their relationship as enacted does not unfairly pressure or limit other staff members' decisions or autonomy— such as Joe and Luisa, even inadvertently, functioning as a "bloc" in terms of larger staff decisions regarding assignments or perks. Depending on a number of institutional or community factors, creating such an arrangement may result in negative reactions, and Mark should consult a number of individuals including the dean about specifics to ensure that any arrangement will have the necessary support to prevail and benefit not only Joe and Luisa but also OSAL and EC. If Joe's and/or Luisa's termination or transfer results from this situation, Mark should agree to serve as a reference if he can provide a positive, balanced, and honest assessment of their work (e.g., ACPA 1.9; NASPA 14; CAS Nonmalfeasance [4], Veracity [1,2,3]).

Mark should initiate a meeting with Joe and Luisa immediately and ask them about what he has heard "through the grapevine." While he might express personal congratulations or pleasure for them as individuals, he should also directly address potential work-related implications of their personal relationship along with any relevant EC policies. If Joe and/or Luisa do not acknowledge or resist discussing work-related implications, Mark should be firm about either following the EC policies or, alternately, the likelihood that he (Mark), possibly in cooperation with the dean and/or another campus office, will be considering appropriate arrangements in light of their relationship. For additional reasons related to their education and professional development, since Joe and Luisa may together or separately face this issue in the future, Mark should also discuss professionals' obligations to inform their supervisors while also acknowledging his recent absence in this particular case. Although Luisa, in particular, has more work experience than Mark, and both Joe and Luisa are older than Mark, Mark should respectfully and appropriately reinforce his status as their supervisor as well as his ethical responsibility ultimately to support and foster their effectiveness as professionals.

Mark should apprise the dean of the situation with respect to work-related considerations. He should also work with the dean as appropriate to follow EC consensual relationship policies, craft a work arrangement in light of the personal relationship, or work to help Joe and/or Luisa determine alternate placements to commence before the end of the year. Mark's decision regarding GA contracts for the following year can be regarded as a separate issue, given the year-to-year nature of the contracts. However, if Mark decides to rehire only one of these current GAs, his decision should not be discriminatory. If Mark decides to rehire both GAs, his decision should be made with full acknowledgement of the range of possible outcomes of intimate relationships and with guarantees from Joe and Luisa of cooperation, honesty, and willingness to place OSAL's effectiveness at the center of their professional concerns.

In Mark's meeting with the dean, it could also become apparent that, while EC may not have a policy addressing consensual intimate relationships among coworkers, the dean does not wish to condone or accommodate staff members engaging in extramarital relationships. The dean's objections may be grounded in personal values or his concerns about the life choices Joe and Luisa as staff members are modeling for EC students. If the dean objects to designing and implementing workplace accommodations for Joe and Luisa, Mark should discuss with the dean the nature and range of his objections as well as the grounds upon which a decision regarding their statuses will be based and any redress or appeal processes that would be available to Luisa and Joe. Mark will then likely face his own choices regarding next steps with Luisa and Joe if he is asked to implement a decision with which he disagrees.

Decision Appraisal

By implementing the strategies above, Mark has a good chance of bringing an ethically responsible resolution to this situation. However, continued monitoring is necessary to ensure that subsequent problems do not arise from his actions or, if they do appear, they are addressed in an ethically responsible manner. Mark's strategies show respect for Joe's and Luisa's autonomy by respecting their decision to enter into an intimate relationship as well as by discussing with them how their decision influences their work and OSAL. His plan promotes justice by applying applicable policies fairly or creating sets of accommodations that are fairly conceived and applied. Mark's strategies benefit others through his consideration of potential impacts for OSAL staff of the intimate relationship.

Mark also benefits others in the institution if the arrangement he creates and implements becomes a precedent that other offices may adapt or apply in future situations, and he benefits Joe and Luisa by helping them understand the work-related ethical implications of otherwise private relationships. In this way, Mark also demonstrates faithfulness to Joe and to Luisa by fulfilling his agreements with them in terms of applying institutional policies or determining appropriate adaptations to their working arrangements. Additionally, Mark is being faithful to the dean by apprising him of the situation and discussing actions with him. Mark's strategies of due confidentiality and respect for Joe's and Luisa's privacy do not contribute to harm, and his application of policies or implementation of work arrangements should be evaluated to ensure that other OSAL staff members are not harmed or disadvantaged.

In addition to honoring the above principles, Mark's strategy will enjoy greater success to the extent that he conducts himself prudently and respectfully and proceeds in accordance with his prior knowledge of people and the institution. For example, Mark's prior effective and respectful supervisory interactions with Joe and with Luisa will help him undertake these potentially sensitive conversations. His prior working relationship with the dean and others on campus, who may have now become relevant to this situation, will also help Mark determine how to best approach the meetings and follow-up contacts that may be involved in pursuing his strategies for resolution.

Contextual Factors

Some additions or changes to the case itself may prompt different interpretations or responses. Below, we list and briefly discuss a number of conditions that may serve to complicate the case and its resolution. Other complications certainly exist, and it would be fruitful to consider these in light of the case interpretations and proposed solutions.

• What if EC were a private, religiously affiliated institution? In this case, the professional ramifications of acknowledging engagement in a consensual extramarital relationship may result in sharply decreased status or effectiveness—if not departure—of one or both staff members. Institutional mission, history, and espoused values of a campus can have profound professional implications for personal behaviors.

• What if EC's policies regarding coworker relationships reflected heterosexual assumptions (e.g., referred to marriage and/or extramarital relationships) and Joe and Luisa were instead Joe and Rob or Luisa and Kate? In this case, Mark should initially try, with guidance from experienced others, to apply the spirit of the existing policies to the situation involving Joe and Rob (or Luisa and Kate) while also voicing his concerns about the apparent policy bias that restricts its usefulness and applicability to everyone. Depending on institutional response to the situation and to Mark's concerns, this could be an example of irreconcilable ethical terrain. Mark may conclude that his personal values and commitments to inclusiveness and equity will not foster his effectiveness in or commitment to this particular campus. These conclusions could constitute ethical grounds for Mark to consider leaving the institution.

• What if either Joe or Luisa were married or in a committed relationship with another person? This circumstance may not matter to some involved in the situation as colleagues or supervisors, but others may be extremely troubled with the infidelity and what it suggests to them about the professional's integrity and faithfulness to agreements or promises in general. Although this circumstance may not fundamentally change the recommendations or strategies outlined above, the individuals' work environment may be characterized by increased distrust and diminished effectiveness, which the supervisor should monitor for future action and the professional should be prepared to face and deal with.

• What if Joe's or Luisa's OSAL work performance thus far had been marginal or substandard? If this were the case, Mark's ongoing formal and informal supervisory interactions should have reflected his concerns and specified improvement goals and accountability measures for follow-up. The degree to which work performance is unacceptable as well as the types of subsequent harm to OSAL may certainly influence Mark's decision to terminate or decline to offer a second-year contract. However, he should be clear about the reasons supporting his actions. Prior poor work performance, however, particularly if it has involved failures to improve or to meet supervisory expectations, can raise questions about a staff member's general degree of professional commitment to the work and to being successful.

• What if staff members or students expressed to Mark their discomfort with Joe's and Luisa's public displays of affection (on campus or off campus)? To the extent that the displays of affection, particularly but not only on campus, can affect work-related effectiveness and the professional status of OSAL, Mark may choose to discuss professional behavior and community norms and perceptions with Joe and Luisa as part of ongoing professional development and supervisory expectations for professionalism. Depending on the individuals expressing this discomfort, Mark may also wish to work with those individuals about how they can communicate their perceptions and potential concerns directly to Joe or Luisa themselves.

• What if, during their initial meeting, the dean asks Mark to terminate Joe and/or Luisa immediately? Particularly if Mark has not yet been able to collect all relevant information, he should resist this suggestion, since information gathering and deliberate due consideration has not been exercised. If, with the benefit of more information, Mark disagrees with the dean's request that he fire Joe and Luisa, Mark should discuss with the dean the grounds for proposed termination as well as other options that are available and, in Mark's view, more desirable. If the dean insists, Mark can refuse to comply and risk his own termination or other work-related consequences. If the dean insists and Mark complies, Mark can consider the consequences, positive or negative, for his effectiveness at OSAL and EC in light of his espoused ethical commitments and his continued reporting relationship to the dean.

• What if an editorial subsequently appears in the campus newspaper calling for Mark, the Dean, and OSAL to "come clean" about the decisions made? The matter described above is a personnel matter and deserving of official confidentiality. Joe's and Luisa's relationship is the subject of "grapevine" talk and possibly a great amount of curiosity on campus, and Joe and Luisa themselves should be the only individuals who are free to share information or not. Ordinarily, Mark should remain silent, and he should have the support of the dean for doing so.

Final Considerations

From the case studies like the one above, identify key points as well as information that is currently missing or needed, but also know that professionals are called to act in situations where they do not have all the information they would prefer, such as in crisis or after-hours situations. For example, Mark might really like to know how, in general, the Dean of Students regards intimate relationships among colleagues (particularly if Mark is tempted or thinks it would be "right" to frame his response or recommendations in accordance with the dean's values), but Mark may not know this information, and the dean may not offer his opinions even if asked. In many ways, the dean is also respecting Mark's autonomy as Joe's and Luisa's supervisor and letting Mark, if not requiring Mark, to think through what is required or entailed in this situation and allowing him an important opportunity for professional growth. Although Mark may not be able yet to answer the dean's ultimate question of what he is going to do, he needs to be prepared to identify the key aspects of a situation and engage in ethically informed discussions about options in light of ethical goals or aims such as respecting autonomy or being fair or just.

As a reminder, the issues in this case and in the other cases are small scale and limited, but this does not mean that these situations or their effective resolutions are unimportant. Unless the situations are handled particularly poorly, they will likely not be publicized in newspapers or web sites or otherwise attract very much external attention. Nonetheless, the outcomes are potentially far reaching. The consequences of the decision in the above situation will affect Joe and Luisa and Mark directly, as Mark handles a potentially delicate supervisory situation and Joe and Luisa learn about balancing professional expectations with personal decisions and choices. The dean is already involved in this situation in terms of requesting resolution, and most of any further internal oversight will occur at Mark's or the dean's level (unless EU policies call for extra-unit monitoring).

However, the outcome of the decision will also indirectly affect students, staff members, and others who are watching to see what happens. On the one hand, curiosity may initially motivate attention to unusual workplace developments, but ethical and professional conduct in all situations communicates and reinforces the degree of confidence students and staff can have in a campus or a unit and its leaders at all levels. Although most campuses and units have mission statements, values or vision statements, and policies, the everyday actions and behaviors by professionals at all levels serve to reinforce and ground the more abstract and publicly proclaimed mission and values.

Finally, successfully or satisfactorily addressing the situations in the case studies will help illuminate larger issues for the professionals themselves, such as understanding the ethical aspects they may tend to emphasize, downplay, or fail to notice, resulting in greater self-awareness of a major component of one's professional identity. As readers work through the following case studies, we suggest that they may wish to discuss these or related situations with others in informal settings as one way of becoming more comfortable with discussions centered on ethics, values, and professional uncertainties. Student affairs professionals have a long and rich tradition of engaging each other in these kinds of conversations, known as "shop talk." Many times when professionals ask a colleague, "Got a minute?" or "Can I buy you some coffee?", what follows is a story (often shortened and made hypothetical) that is unusual or perplexing and a request for the colleague's input, perspectives, and assistance in helping identify warranted and workable options. Through these informal interactions, professionals can also support each other to try to be as ethical, self-aware, and responsible as possible.

3

Academic Student Services Cases

Advising from the Heart and Head

Ray Quirolgico
University of San Francisco

Mark is an Academic Advisor in the Department of Learning Resources at Lakeville University (LU), a midsized, private, urban university with comprehensive undergraduate and graduate programs. Learning Resources provides academic advising for undeclared students as well as tutoring, workshops, and individual assistance with academic success strategies, such as time management and study skills. Most of Mark's advisees are undergraduates in the School of Arts and Sciences, although he has done outreach to the Schools of Engineering, Education, and Business as well. Mark is also the faculty advisor for the Lesbian, Gay, Bisexual, and Transgender Student Union (LGBTSU) on campus. This is his first time advising a club on campus, and he is looking forward to interacting with students in a different context than his usual advising appointments. Last year, in his first year of employment at LU, Mark was encouraged by his supervisor to participate in and investigate different organizations on campus so that he could learn more about student life. Mark enjoyed the dynamic energy of the LGBTSU meetings he attended, and the students asked him to be their club's faculty advisor in Mark's second semester of work at this campus (their former advisor, a faculty member, was leaving LU). During his relatively short tenure at this campus, Mark has observed many students come to the organizational meetings and find a comfortable niche on the LU campus. The students involved in LGBTSU seem very happy and sociable, and LGBTSU has facilitated some well-attended and well-received educational and social programs on campus. Several students who have served in LGBTSU leadership capacities have also subsequently volunteered as student leaders in orientation, residence life, and student government, among others.

Mark has seen particular growth in one student, Seth. Seth is a 19-year old sophomore who is also the first in his family to attend college. During the past semester, Seth declared an economics major and enrolled in the School of Business. Seth also had recently come to terms with his sexuality and started attending LGBTSU meetings and events. At first, he was very shy and rarely spoke. As time went on, he became a natural leader for the group and was elected vice president within a short period of time. Mark congratulated Seth after his election, and Seth responded, "I finally feel like I've found a place where I belong. Being involved in this group is what keeps me going and what I like most about being at Lakeville. I really can't remember a time when I felt this happy." Mark couldn't have been more pleased for Seth.

One day, when Mark went to the Learning Resources lobby to meet a student for an advising appointment, he noticed Seth in the lobby waiting to see an advisor. Because other students were ahead of Seth on the sign-in sheet for walk-in assistance, Seth ended up visiting with Ann, a colleague of Mark's. Later that day, Mark asked Ann if everything was okay with Seth.

Ann told Mark that Seth was in some academic difficulty, since his cumulative GPA had fallen below 2.0. Ann continued, "From his high school record, it looks like Seth has struggled academically for awhile. There's been some improvement since coming to LU, but he needs to clean up some incompletes and work on his academic skills. We've set up a plan to help him with study skills. I also recommended that he devote much more time to his academics, once he told me how involved he's been with student groups and such. I'm afraid that these involvements are distracting him from concentrating on his coursework. As this semester goes on, I've asked him to keep me posted on how his courses are going. He may need to start looking at other majors if his grades aren't high enough to stay in business, since economics has a high GPA requirement for acceptance into the program. Seth thinks he's on track to bring his grades up and really doesn't want to cut back on his extracurriculars, but we'll see how things go."

Mark was aware from his club advisor training through the Student Activities Office that officers of student organizations must carry at least a full time load each semester and must carry a minimum 2.0 cumulative GPA. While student organization advisors are supposed to receive grade reports of their officers each semester from the Student Activities Office, the former LGBTSU advisor said this hadn't happened for the last couple of years due to staffing cutbacks and reassignment of duties. Mark knew that Seth had also recently agreed to take on some major programming and outreach commitments with LGBTSU in addition to his responsibilities as vice president.

What should Mark do and why?

The Case of the Pressuring Parents

Justina Grubor
University of Maryland—College Park

Phil is an academic advisor for undecided students at Grantland University, a large, public research institution in the Southeast. Phil's job is to assist students with the process of completing their general education requirements and choosing a major. After students choose a major, they are assigned a new advisor in their academic departments. When helping students explore majors, one of Phil's primary concerns is helping students choose majors that will allow them to be academically successful. In this role, he encourages students to assess their academic strengths and weaknesses as part of the decision-making process.

At Grantland, undecided first-year students are required to meet with their advisors twice a semester during their first two semesters. In these meetings, advisors assist students with course planning for the following semester and assess students' academic progress and adjustment to college. Advisors also inform students who are experiencing difficulties about appropriate campus resources available to them.

To assist first-year students and advisors with monitoring students' academic progress, the registrar's office compiles and distributes midterm grade reports for all first-year students. Just after grade reports were issued in mid-October, Ross, a first-semester student, came to Phil's office for one of his mandatory academic advising meetings. During orientation in August, Ross had expressed an interest in engineering, so Phil had suggested he take an introductory calculus class that would meet the engineering college's requirements. However, Ross received an unsatisfactory grade report for the class to date. He said to Phil, "Maybe I should drop the class, because I might end up failing it. But if I drop calculus, it will be hard for me to go on with the preengineering courses, and I may have to pick another major."

When Phil asked Ross if finding a tutor for his calculus class would be helpful, Ross shook his head and said, "It might, but the problem is that I think I want to be a psychology major, but I'm taking calculus because my parents want me to be an engineer. If I don't major in something like engineering, my folks have said they'll stop paying my tuition. I get some student loans, and I work part-time, but without their help, it would be really hard for me to stay in school."

When Phil asked Ross to tell him more about the situation, Ross replied, "Well, neither of my parents attended college—they never had that chance—but they really wanted both my sister and me to go to college, so we could get good paying jobs. They've already cut off my sister, because she's decided to major in philosophy. She's had to cut back to part-time courses and work full time in a book and music store to support herself and pay tuition. My folks told me, 'You can't make the same mistake she made!'"

Ross concluded that he feels pressured to choose a major that will please his parents, but he doubts that psychology will be acceptable, even though he really likes the introductory psychology course he's taking now and he received an A minus on his midterm report.

When Phil asked Ross how he can be helpful, Ross said,

"I really do want to stay here as a student, so what would really help is if you could talk to my parents and let them know that I'm on track and that this calculus grade isn't a big deal and won't hurt me. They might listen to you; I'm not sure they'll listen to me if I try to tell them this. This would give me some time to figure this out and decide what to do."

What should Phil do and why?

When the Golden Child Becomes the Problem Employer

Alana Jardis
University of Puget Sound

W. Houston Dougharty
Lewis and Clark College

One of Chris's responsibilities as a career counselor at Midamerica State University (a large, comprehensive research university of 28,000 students, located in a midsize city in the upper Midwest) is to coordinate employer relations for a number of visiting organizations and assist individual students with career counseling and placement-related concerns. Chris is the designated office contact for Marshall-Howarth Pharmaceuticals (MPH), a large, high-profile, privately held regional employer. MHP annually hosts a well-attended evening information session prior to a day of on-campus interviews with interested MSU students. When Chris arrived at her office the morning of MHP's campus interviews, she retrieved a voicemail from Jenn, an MSU senior who attended the informational session the night before. Jenn left an emotional message for Chris at 10 p.m. In her message, Jenn said, "Chris, I had to call and let you know how incredibly uncomfortable I was tonight at the Marshall-Howarth Pharmaceuticals information session. I can't even tell you how frustrated and angry I am about this experience. I'm seriously thinking of dropping out of the interview process."

Jenn went on to say that the formal presentation about Marshall-Howarth was excellent and appealing. However, later over coffee, the employer's representative was informally discussing company culture with students. Jenn said, "I think his name was Todd, and he said that they don't usually expect the tenure of female employees to be too long, because they know that many of them will stop working to have families and that they supported that choice. He said that he believed it was important for women to be wives and mothers and that a woman should seriously consider staying home with her children in order to raise them in a more values-driven manner."

Jenn's voice message continued, "I really thought that was inappropriate, and I'm disappointed and outraged that the campus would support and endorse an employer who is so overtly sexist. I think your office needs to reconsider whether Marshall-Howarth should be allowed to recruit at MSU. I'm also going to speak with MSU's Women's Center director—I think she needs to hear about this, too."

Even though this was only Chris's second year in the position, she knew that MHP had long tradition of supporting the Career Center and MSU and hired a large number of MSU graduates each year. In addition, she knew that the company representative who had been scheduled to present the information session was Todd Wheelock. Todd is a well-known and respected Midamerica alumnus who had been MSU's student government president five years earlier and currently serves on MSU's Alumni Board. Todd frequently returns to campus and visits classes in the business school as a representative of his company and his profession of accounting. On two separate occasions, Chris has overheard the business school dean refer to Todd as "our golden child."

As Chris hung up the phone, she noticed that Todd has arrived to prepare for his day of interviews—the first of which was scheduled in 45 minutes with Jenn. Dr. Cheryl Forbes, the career center's director and long-time friend of MHP, walked past Chris's office to greet Todd warmly, asking, "How did things go last night? It's always so great to have you back on campus, Todd!"

Chris heard Dr. Forbes' secretary whisper, "Dr. Forbes, the Women's Center director is on line one. She says it's urgent."

While Todd walked down the hallway toward his assigned interview room and the director went to her office, Jenn knocked on Chris's door and said, "I know I'm here early for my interview appointment. Did you get my phone message from last night?"

What should Chris do and why?

GPA Calculations

Becky Vianden
University of Arkansas-Fayetteville

As a second-year academic advisor, Tony knows that the policy at Brush Creek College, a small tribal college in the Southwest, stipulates a student's academic dismissal if his or her cumulative GPA remains under 2.0 for four consecutive semesters. At the beginning of this semester when Tony met with Sam, a junior, Tony informed Sam that he was in jeopardy of being academically dismissed, since his cumulative GPA had been under a 2.0 for three semesters in a row.

Tony then used a GPA calculation worksheet to help Sam set academic goals for the semester and to determine what grades he needed in order to raise his cumulative GPA above 2.0. Based on this formula, Tony concluded that Sam needed to earn nothing lower than two Cs and two Bs in his four courses (three credits each) this semester. Sam guaranteed Tony that he would make the necessary academic changes, saying, "I promise that I'll get this done, Tony. I appreciate your help, and I'm really serious about staying here and getting my degree. I know that I've dug a deep hole for myself with my grades, but if I can get back on track and graduate, I think I can make a good case for getting into medical school or something similar. This is a new plan for me, but I really want to provide medical services on some level for people in my tribe. There's such a huge need."

On the Friday of finals week, Sam came to Tony's office. Sam had checked his semester grades online, and he came to tell Tony that he got just what he needed: two Bs and two Cs. Tony congratulated Sam. They discussed briefly Sam's course load for next semester, and then Sam left. Tony reviewed his records and made notes about Sam's visit. He accessed Sam's transcript online to verify Sam's grades and saw two Bs and two Cs, but the entry for Sam's cumulative GPA remained just below 2.0. Puzzled, Tony glanced over the GPA calculation sheet he used with Sam at the beginning of the semester and saw with a sinking heart that he had made a miscalculation. In order to avoid academic dismissal, Sam really needed to get no less than one C and three Bs. Because of Tony's miscalculation, Sam will be academically dismissed.

Tony immediately told his supervisor Sharon what happened. She empathized with Tony's situation and asked to see Sam's most recent semester transcript. As she reviewed the online record, she told Tony not to worry about it, "You did what you did in good faith. It was just a mistake. I think I can take care of this."

Tony asked, "Shouldn't I get in touch with Sam? I feel awful that this happened."

Sharon said, "No, not yet. Let me check into some options first."

Two weeks later when Tony got a list of his advisees who had been academically dismissed for the new semester, he noted that Sam's name was not on the list. He pulled up Sam's transcript file and saw that one of his C grades from last semester was now a B and that his cumulative GPA was now just above 2.0. The B was from Professor Jones, a faculty member whose nickname among many Brush Creek students was "Easy Al."

Early the next semester, Sam came to see Tony and said, "Did you see my higher grade from last semester? I really didn't think I could do as well as a B in Dr. Jones's class, but I did it. Maybe I should think about trying some of these advanced life science classes, since it looks like I'm back on track with my grades. What do you think?"

What should Tony do and why?

Handpicking Students

Mark Peltz
Luther College

Jim is in his second year as an associate director of the Career Development Office (CDO) within Central State University's (CSU) School of Business. CSU is a public research university with a total student enrollment of more than 38,000. Although Central State University has a centralized career center that serves the entire campus community (both undergraduate and graduate), CSU's professional schools of business, law, and medicine maintain their own career centers to work with graduate students on internship and job placement issues. Working exclusively with the 400 graduate students in the School of Business, Jim, his two associate director colleagues Shawn and Lindsey, and Sarah, a receptionist/recruiting coordinator, all report to the new director Mike, who is completing his first month on the job. As a previous corporate marketing and sales executive, Mike has pledged to increase the number and caliber of employers that visit campus to recruit MBA students. The business school's dean and faculty have expressed strong support for Mike's plans.

As the CDO staff convened for their weekly staff meeting, Mike informed everyone of some very exciting news. Upon his return from an extended trip with the business school's dean to visit a number of Fortune 500 companies, Mike received an offer from one particular company (which happens to be headed by a former business client of Mike's) to fly five of CSU's graduating MBA students to New York for on-site interviews. These students will be considered for positions offering very attractive salaries and benefits. Mike continued, "Now, we need to decide which of our students will go. I want each of you to go through the students you've worked with this past year and give me the names of five graduating students who you think will give the best impression. I'll compare everyone's lists and make the final decision. I'm also going to ask some faculty members for their input as well."

Shawn, another associate director, asked, "Shouldn't we post the opportunity and have students submit their resumes for consideration like we do with other job opportunities? Then the company could decide who they want to interview."

Jim, Lindsey, and Sarah tentatively nodded their heads in agreement, but Mike angrily retorted, "Absolutely not. This opportunity is too important. It is critical that we put our most polished students in front of these executives, and anyway, we don't have time. This is not negotiable; give me your lists by the end of the day."

What should Jim do and why?

Going to Bat for Your Students

Corey Rumann
Iowa State University

Frank is a 26-year-old career and transfer advisor in the Student Development Center at Windy Meadows Community College. Windy Meadows is a two-year college of 2,000 students in a small, rural, Western community of 7,000. Frank just completed his first year on the job, and he is excited about how well things have been going for him there. He's also looking forward to not being so busy at work during the summer months. Frank's primary responsibilities in the Student Development Center are to assist students with transferring to four-year schools and assist students with their career choices.

During the spring semester, Frank worked as the career and transfer advisor for a student named Tom, assisting him in finding an appropriate school to transfer to following completion of his associate's degree at Windy Meadows and to further explore his career options in the field of education after graduation. Tom is a 28-year-old student who began attending Windy Meadows over three years ago, and he had hoped to graduate by now. However, after successfully completing his first semester at the school with a 3.5 GPA, his National Guard unit was deployed to a combat zone for an 18-month tour of duty. Tom subsequently completed another year of college, and he very much wants to graduate following the upcoming fall semester, so he can move on to a four-year university. Prior to starting college, Tom worked in oil fields until he realized his passion was to become a teacher.

Frank joined the city softball league, and Tom was on his team. The team often went out after games to local establishments to play darts or pool and talk. Tom and Frank became friendly, and Tom confided in Frank that his adjustment back to civilian life had been difficult at best since his unit returned from overseas. He often experienced nightmares and felt anxious much of the time. Tom's grades also had suffered because of this, and he voiced concern about not being able to graduate, because Windy Meadows has a policy that if students earn below a 2.0 GPA for two consecutive semesters, they must sit out one semester before reenrolling. Frank also knew Tom's wife, Sandy, because she worked at a popular restaurants in town. Sandy also was concerned about Tom's well being and shared those concerns with Frank.

One day, Tom came to Frank's office and said, "I need you to do me a favor, Frank. I just received a letter from the college, and they are suspending me for a semester because of my grades. I need you to go to bat for me. I know the last couple of semesters have been rough, but I'm sure I can make up the classes I didn't pass and still graduate in December. Anyway, if I sit out a semester I know I will have to go back to work in the oil fields, and I'll never become a teacher."

Frank looked at Tom inquisitively and asked "Why me?"

"Because you're the only one here who really knows all I've been going through the last couple of years," Tom replied. Frank knew from his experiences as a hall director working with students that consistency is the best policy, but in this case, an exception seemed appropriate. Frank looked at Tom and said, "Okay, I'll recommend you be placed on academic probation rather than suspension on one condition."

"Anything," Tom said.

Frank continued, "You have to go see the college counselor or a local community counselor to get some help for those nightmares and your anxiety."

"No problem at all," Tom replied. "You have a deal."

As part of the appeal process, the Student Appeals Board at Windy Meadows allowed college personnel to write letters on a student's behalf if the staff member believed the student would take advantage of being placed on academic probation rather than being suspended from the school altogether.

Frank wrote a letter supporting Tom, and based on Frank's strong recommendation, the Student Appeals Board granted Tom's request to be placed on academic probation rather than being suspended.

In the middle of the fall semester, midterm grades came out. Frank had access to those grades, and he saw that Tom had not made satisfactory progress. Frank also knew that Tom had not gone to see a counselor, because Sandy told Frank that was the case when he stopped at the restaurant for lunch the other day.

Frank had messages from both the Dean of Students and the Dean of Instruction to call them in regard to Tom's status. Frank is torn about what to do. He really felt like he was doing a good thing, and he truly believes Tom is a good student who is just going through a rough time. In addition, Frank is noticing that other students who were in Tom's National Guard unit are starting to come to him asking for his intervention in regard to their academic status at the college.

What should Frank do and why?

A Numbers Game

Kevin J. Hardy
Iowa State University

After graduating from his master's program in higher education this past spring, Lucas accepted a position in the Engineering Career Center at Desert State University (DSU), a large, research science and technology focused institution in the Southwest. The College of Engineering has approximately 4,000 students, including graduate students, and the Career Center provides a variety of services, including a large career fair. Lucas and many of his colleagues are responsible for coordinating the fair, and Lucas has been looking forward to this project, since it was something that was highlighted as an important part of his position during his interview.

Companies were invited to participate in the career fair, where they would collect resumes, visit with potential interns and employees, and showcase their companies. The registrations arrived quickly after invitations were sent. By the deadline, Lucas had received registrations from 230 companies.

Madeline, his supervisor, was thrilled, "Lucas, this is great news! This is a record number of company registrations for the fair; last year we only had 212 companies. It's great for our students, and it's important to the college's national rankings, too."

Lucas worked with his colleagues to make logistical arrangements for the career fair, and the fair was a great success. Students visited the career center to have their resumes reviewed and discuss opportunities that might be presented at the career fair prior to the event, and Lucas and his colleagues felt confident that the students were well-prepared for the fair. Representatives from the companies were complimentary about the coordination of the event as well. After the fair, a number of students stopped by Lucas' office to tell him how helpful the fair was for them. One senior said, "I've gone to this since I was a freshman, looking for internships and now looking for a full-time job. This was by far the best coordinated of all of the career fairs I've attended here."

Despite all the positive comments, Lucas was disappointed that of the 230 companies that registered for space at the fair, representatives from only 192 companies attended the event. Having almost 40 no-show companies was a concern, and Lucas knew that 192 was not the record number Madeline was so enthusiastically anticipating.

When putting together the final report on the project, Lucas shared with Madeline, "I think the event was a great success. I've had lots of positive feedback. Unfortunately, our registration numbers didn't play out as expected. Instead of 230 companies, we only had 192. But students were really pleased with the fair, so the numbers probably don't matter so much."

Madeline congratulated Lucas, and said, "I've heard great things about the fair, too. You should be pleased; it was very successful. However, when we report the numbers, you need to indicate that 230 companies registered and leave it at that."

Shortly afterward, Lucas received a call from Caretta Lawrence, the Assistant to the dean of engineering. Caretta said, "Lucas, Dean Oliver was very pleased to hear about the success of the career fair, especially given the record number of companies. She plans to send letters to all 230 companies to thank them for visiting DSU's College of Engineering. Will you please send me an electronic file with that contact information this afternoon? I called Madeline earlier, and she told me that you'd have all this information. Oh, and I'm preparing a press release about the career fair's success, too. The press release will go out toward the end of the week."

Lucas thought about these conversations as he was finishing his report. 230 registrations were made for the career fair; that was certainly accurate. But only 192 companies were represented, and Madeline was insistent that he report only the registrations.

What should Lucas do and why?

Peer Advising Program

Juan R. Guardia
Florida State University

Industrial State University (ISU) is a large, private, comprehensive university located in a major city in the southwestern United States. ISU is well known for its journalism and communications programs and has been successful in placing graduates in broadcasting, newspaper, and public relations positions. The academic advising center in the School of Journalism and Mass Communication assists majors and prospective majors. It is staffed by a director, three academic advisors, and four undergraduate peer advisors. Because of the popularity of the school, enrollment in its seven majors is limited, and admission requirements include a personal interview.

Elaine is in her first year as an academic advisor in the School of Journalism and Mass Communication (JMC) at ISU and is one of three full-time advisors in the center. Along with her advising duties, her responsibilities include supervising the four undergraduate peer advisors. The duties of peer advisors include assisting prospective JMC students with prerequisite course selection and the school's application process. Because peer advisors assist students with course selection, they have limited access to student academic records.

One Wednesday during the fall semester, Elaine asked to speak with Marie, the director of academic advising, regarding Nina, a senior peer advisor. Elaine described how Nina had been late to work on several occasions and her work attitude had become poor. Elaine continued, "I started documenting these problems two months ago, and I've met with Nina formally on two occasions about these. She gets better for awhile with being on time, but her attitude continues to be lackluster in her work with prospective students. Yesterday, I also noticed through routine audits of our tracking software that Nina has accessed academic and transcript records for four students who haven't registered with us as prospects. I am really concerned about this recent development as well, and I recommend that we terminate her. I don't want her performance to start affecting the other peer advisors."

Marie asked, "So do you believe that she's been given adequate opportunity to improve?"

When Elaine nodded yes, Marie expressed her support for Elaine's decision to fire Nina, but added, "But I must say that I'm somewhat surprised. The former academic advisor who supervised the peer staff had never reported problems with Nina's performance in the last two years. But you clearly have the documentation that would justify terminating her."

Elaine thanked Marie for her support and told her she would convey the news to Nina. The following day, Elaine met with Nina to inform her that she would be let go due to poor job performance. Upset and angry, Nina asked if there was anything she could do to stay on as a peer advisor. Elaine told her that the decision was final.

When Elaine arrived to work the following Monday, she noticed Nina working in the center. Marie called Elaine into her office quickly and said, "Nina appealed her termination to me on Friday, and I must say she convinced me to give her a second chance. She has assured me that she will improve, and her attitude does seem quite positive today. Also, two of the other peer advisors approached me last Friday specifically to say how helpful Nina's advising experience has been for them when they've had questions."

What should Elaine do and why?

Illegal Work

Eric Comins
University at Buffalo

Kelsey is in her second year as an international student advisor at Maplewood University, a large, public research university in a city of almost 50,000 people. The university enrolls approximately 30,000 students. Kelsey reports to the director of International Student Services (ISS). Kelsey, the director, another advisor, and a clerical staff member serve this fairly large population of international students, approximately 3,500 students from 100 different countries.

ISS policy has always been to encourage international students to adhere to all stipulations of their F-1 nonimmigrant student status. One of these provisions governs off-campus work for students with F-1 status. Essentially, any off-campus work by these students must be approved before the work begins. Work experience can be authorized by ISS if it is a necessary component of the student's academic program or authorized by the USCIS (formerly known as the INS) if the proposed work is optional but related to the student's major. The USCIS penalties for unauthorized work by F-1 nonimmigrant status holders are severe and can include deportation.

While Kelsey was out for dinner one night with a group of friends, she noticed Ian, one of the international students at Maplewood University, working in the restaurant, although she was not certain that he saw her. Kelsey didn't know all of the international students at Maplewood, but it would be difficult for her not to know Ian. He was an officer in one international student club, served as a mentor for new international students, and had helped organize Maplewood's most recent international fair. As the principal staff member who processes off-campus work requests, Kelsey didn't think that Ian had applied for work authorization. Furthermore, working as a server would not be related to his major, computer science. In the past, some of her MU colleagues have mentioned that they thought they saw some of the university's international students working off-campus in certain restaurants, but Kelsey never actually witnessed such an occurrence until now.

The following morning, Ian approached Kelsey in her office as soon as the ISS doors open, begging her not to report his employment. She said, "Ian, do you realize how serious, as well as illegal, it is for you to be working off-campus without prior authorization?"

Ian explained, "I have to work at the restaurant to pay for my education. You know that international students have to pay higher tuition to come to this school. Besides that, my grandfather is very ill back in my country, and he has paid for most of my education so far. Since he's been sick, I had to find a way to pay for school."

Since he was within 18 months of graduation, Ian did not want to return to his home country without a degree, especially after the investment he had already made. Normally a very stoic and steady person, Ian got tears in his eyes and said, "Kelsey, I don't know what else to do!"

What should Kelsey do and why?

Ability to Handle a Disability

Lori Patton
Iowa State University

Connie is in her third year as the assistant director of publications for the Office of Family Programs in the Division of Student Affairs at Logan College. Logan College is a private baccalaureate institution with a population of 8,500 students. Palomino State University (PSU), located twenty minutes north, has a student affairs master's program in which enrolled students either work at PSU or at a neighboring college like Logan. Throughout the years, several PSU master's students have completed two-year assistantships in student affairs offices at Logan College.

In advertising her assistantship opening last spring, Connie worked with the coordinator of PSU's student affairs program but unfortunately had no luck hiring a graduate assistant for the upcoming academic year. Connie knew that she could not go without assistance this year, as her office was responsible for communicating frequently with students' families via a newsletter, a web site, and e-mails, as well as helping coordinate some campus events for family members. She decided to hire a senior at Logan to assist her once fall classes had begun.

Just prior to the start of classes, Donovan, who was admitted late to PSU's master's program, contacted her about an assistantship. Connie arranged an interview and asked that he submit a writing sample and resume. Prior to the interview, Connie read the writing sample and decided that his writing was okay but would need improvement. When they met, Donovan explained his experience and interest in the position. Connie reviewed a hard copy of the position description and verbally outlined her expectations with Donovan. She carefully explained that the position, among other things, required attention to detail, strong organizational skills, and effective writing skills. Donovan expressed his understanding of the responsibilities and his confidence in his ability to handle the job. Relieved, Connie decided to make the offer, and Donovan accepted. He began work the following day.

Connie provided Donovan with on-going training and assigned him several projects. Throughout August, she met with Donovan weekly, explained what needed to be done, and provided timelines for his projects—some of which would be due the next month. One afternoon in early September, Connie noted that a deadline was fast approaching for the upcoming family weekend. Donovan was responsible for ensuring that personalized letters of invitation were sent to the parents of each student. Connie decided to check on Donovan's progress but saw that he had already left for the day. As she walked past his desk, she noticed that Donovan had printed out several family weekend invitation letters on office letterhead. She also saw a stack of envelopes that had been addressed. Connie glanced at the top letter and noticed several typographical errors. She looked closer and saw that the letter was poorly structured. She realized that, although she and Donovan had discussed the general content of the invitation letter, he had not shared a draft with her. Thinking quickly, Connie called the campus's central mail office and asked whether all of that afternoon's outgoing mail from her office could be intercepted. The supervisor asked her to wait, and then he returned to the phone: "Okay, we have your batch here. We hadn't processed it yet. I can have this brought to your office tomorrow morning, okay?" Connie agreed and thanked him.

The next morning, Connie looked through the retrieved mail and saw that about two dozen of Donovan's invitation letters had been in yesterday's outgoing batch of mail. As soon as Donovan arrived, Connie asked him about the letters on his desk and the outgoing mail. Donovan replied, "Oh, yeah, I've made such good progress with this that I was able to start sending out letters yesterday. Family weekend is coming up so quickly, and I wanted us to get a jump on the invitations so that we could focus on the events that we'll be planning."

Connie said, "But you should have shown me the letter you were working on." She went on to explain that she had seen the letters on his desk and had been able to intercept the outgoing mail. After Donovan verified that no other letters had been sent prior to yesterday, Connie continued, "You have to be sure that you've proofread the letters and that I have a chance to see the final copy before any correspondence is sent. If we send out letters with typos and grammatical errors to parents, what kind of impression do you think they'll have of the institution their children are attending? Besides that, what would they think of the quality of our office? This letter really isn't reflective of the writing sample that you had given me when you interviewed."

Connie then went through the letter itself with Donovan, highlighting and explaining items for correction. Donovan grew increasingly red-faced and said, "I'm sorry. I was only trying to expedite things for us. I will do a better job." He got up to leave and turned to add, "My girlfriend did help me with the writing sample that I gave you, but it was still my work. I just wanted her to help me make it more polished."

On subsequent occasions when Connie reviewed his work, she continued to find typographical and grammatical errors on the web site and in e-mails, as well as work that did not reflect the final corrections she had given to Donovan. When Connie discussed these concerns with Donovan, he became increasingly sullen and accused Connie of micro-managing his work and not being supportive while he tried hard to learn the job. "I've just never worked in a place like this before," he said angrily.

In her next meeting with Robert, the director of family programs and Connie's supervisor, she expressed her growing frustration with Donovan's performance and inability to do the work satisfactorily. She asked for Robert's advice on how she should handle the situation.

After hearing everything, Robert agreed that Donovan was not a good fit for the position and that he should seek other employment. Connie notified Donovan of his dismissal, saying that he could keep the assistantship only through the end of fall term. Donovan became visibly upset and accused Connie of not being patient enough. Connie replied, "Donovan, I met with you every week and very specifically went over each assignment with you. We talked about the importance of the details of this job, about the proofreading issue, and the accuracy and professionalism that must be reflected in all of our written materials. I gave you feedback and tried to help you. I'm not sure how much more patient or supportive I could be!" Connie also notified PSU's student affairs graduate program coordinator of the situation, in the hopes that his termination from the assistantship wouldn't unduly jeopardize Donovan's student status or her own prior good relations with the graduate program.

Early in January, as Connie was sorting through applications from Logan seniors to fill the vacant position in her office, Donovan called to request a meeting with Connie, and she agreed. At their meeting, Donovan shared that he had recently registered with the Disability Services Office at PSU, since he had a learning disability that affects his writing abilities and attention span. He continued, "I really have a much better sense of what these problems are now, and I want to ask about the possibility of being rehired. Also, I've looked and looked, and there are no assistantship positions available this spring." This was the first Connie had heard about his learning disability, and she had had no previous experience working with or supervising someone with a learning disability.

What should Connie do and why?

4

Enrollment Services Cases

Snake Grants Program

Matt Brown
Iowa Student Loan Liquidity Corporation

Snake State University (SSU) is a large, public research university located on the Boulder River in the western United States. SSU enrolls 29,000 students, including a sizeable proportion of first-generation students from small mining towns or migrant farmwork backgrounds. Like many comparably sized institutions, SSU has a financial aid director, five associate and assistant directors with varying levels of full-time experience, and a paraprofessional staff of nine graduate assistants.

Within the Student Affairs Division, William, the director of the Office of Student Financial Aid (OSFA), has considerable autonomy to oversee highly specialized areas such as student loans, student employment, scholarship awards, and allocation of university dollars for need-based grants.

The Snake Grants program—dedicated university funds to provide grants to SSU students with unmet financial need—came up at one particular staff meeting held midway through the fall semester. Like all OSFA staff meetings, this meeting had been convened by the director, and all assistant and associate directors were in attendance. Graduate assistants did not attend staff meetings and, instead, covered office phones and met with students during that time. The director always attempted to keep staff meetings as short as possible so that the graduate assistants would not be left without backup for too long.

Susan is the newest addition to SSU's OSFA professional staff. She's an assistant director in her first year of full-time work following graduation with her master's degree; plus, she has two years of financial aid experience as a graduate assistant. She listened as William shared good news with the staff, "Because of record fall enrollment numbers, an additional one-time allocation of $200,000 has been given to OSFA. The allocation has been earmarked for the Snake Grants program and must be expended before the end of the current semester. We need to be sure SSU students can afford to stay here now that they've enrolled."

Zoe, the associate director responsible for the Snake Grants program, instructed all staff members to keep in mind the extra resources that were now available to current students who had unmet financial need and/or outstanding university bills. "If you know students who appear to be candidates for Snake Grant dollars," she said, "drop me an e-mail with their names, their student ID numbers, and brief descriptions of their situations. I'll take it from there."

Susan looked around the room and saw her colleagues nodding and making notes to themselves. She thought quickly of some students she worked with in late summer who took out large loans on top of their modest Snake Grants in order to attend SSU. She also thought about some other admitted students she had seen during the summer. For these students, the SSU financial aid package had not been sufficient for them to enroll without incurring loan debt; most of them had subsequently told her that they would have to attend the local community college instead. Susan furrowed her brow and tried to focus on the meeting, since staff members were already discussing the next agenda item.

What should Susan do and why?

No Time Like the Present

Matt Brown
Iowa Student Loan Liquidity Corporation

Whisper Falls College is a small liberal arts college in the city of Springbrook that is celebrating its 100th year. More than 75% of Whisper Falls's students are state residents, and almost 90% of its alumni have remained in the state after graduation. Over the years, Springbrook has grown into the largest metropolitan community in the state. Like many tuition-driven independent colleges, Whisper Falls has struggled to keep student costs competitive with the land-grant university and community colleges in the area. The college recently added evening and weekend courses in an attempt to attract more adult students. Although some students enroll part-time at Whisper Falls, the Admissions Office has targeted individuals seeking a personalized learning environment for full-time study. Three Admissions representatives are assigned to the surrounding area, allowing the college to be heavily represented at college and career fairs as well as a broad range of community and high school events. Admissions representatives maintain careful records of their contacts, follow-ups, and yields in light of their yearly enrollment targets, and each works closely with prospective students until the beginning of fall classes to ensure maximum enrollment at Whisper Falls.

Simon, the associate director of financial aid at Whisper Falls, has been at the college since completing his master's degree there about two years ago. His first year had passed in a whirlwind of adjusting to the small college culture, and he had also begun his position late, in October. Last August, Simon had his first experience with New Student Day, a welcome and orientation program for new Whisper Falls students held the Friday prior to the start of fall classes. During the week preceding New Student Day, Admissions representatives brought a number of students to his office to visit about financial aid.

As Simon met with students, he was surprised at how many of them had initiated their admission applications that same day and had not yet filed the Free Application for Federal Student Aid (FAFSA), which can be filed and processed as early as January 1 for enrollment in the fall semester of the same year.

Simon carefully explained to each student in this situation, "I will try my very best to project an estimate and create an award letter that will ultimately cover your tuition, which at Whisper Falls is $13,000, and educational expenses. Keep in mind that most colleges, including Whisper Falls, request that financial aid applications be submitted before April first. Timing is everything: we award institutional scholarships and grants on a first-come, first-served basis, a policy shared by many federal and state scholarships and grants. When the grant money is gone, we are forced to include more student loans in your financial aid award offer. Some of the loans are guaranteed by the federal government without credit approval. Other loan options are subject to credit approval and carry origination fees and somewhat higher interest rates. As you might expect, the credit approval loans require more processing time, and we rarely see loan disbursements in less than three weeks from the time you submit your separate application. This is a serious issue, because your first semester tuition and fees are due at the end of the first week of classes."

Simon paused to allow all of the information he had just shared with the student sink in. Then, sounding as optimistic as he could, Simon added that Whisper Falls had customarily extended the payment date for students who qualified for financial aid but whose loan funds had not yet been disbursed.

"We can wait," he said, "but we can't guarantee you will be approved for all of the student loans you might need to pay your bill and cover other education-related expenses."

Over the summer, Simon had looked closely at Whisper Falls's enrollments and withdrawals during the past academic year and the financial aid implications for students and the college. He noticed that about half of the students who had withdrawn before the end of fall semester were students who had filed initial applications for financial aid in August. He also noted that most of these students had withdrawn from Whisper Falls later than the first Friday of classes, after which date only partial tuition refunds were issued. He called the registrar and discovered that most of the departing students had indicated "financial reasons" as the main factor in their decisions to withdraw.

Retention and enrollment issues were becoming even more salient for Whisper Falls this year. Following last spring's board decision to keep tuition rates the same, the Admissions Office was under increased pressure to attract and enroll even more students for the fall. The summer was going fast, and New Student Day was quickly approaching.

As was customary, Simon and his other financial aid colleague had cleared their calendars in anticipation of drop-in meetings with students and family members throughout the day. Shortly after 8 a.m. on New Student Day, Simon looked up to see Cheryl, one of the Admission representatives assigned to the Springbrook area, saying good morning and ushering a person into Simon's office. Simon greeted Cheryl and the new student, who Cheryl introduced with a broad smile as "Patricia, Whisper Falls's newest full-time student."

Simon invited Patricia to sit down, and Cheryl said, "Patricia is all ready to enroll in fall classes. She just needs a quick overview of her anticipated financial aid package. Also, could you help her with filing her FAFSA form?" Cheryl smiled again and left.

Simon turned to Patricia, who shook her head gently, smiled, and said, "This is all happening very quickly. Cheryl kept in touch with me after I went to a career fair last November, but I just recently decided to give college a try. No one in my family ever went to college, but I want to set a better example for my two sons who are in middle school. No one at my high school 15 years ago ever told a young Black woman like me that I had what it takes to go to college, and I want it to be different for my sons. When I talked to Cheryl, she said that the grant and loan programs will take care of everything. I hope that that's the case, because I feel like I have a whole lot riding on this decision."

What should Simon do and why?

Life on the Road

W. Houston Dougharty
Lewis and Clark College

Jackie is in her first year on the admission staff of her alma mater Westergrove University, a small, comprehensive, very selective university of 5,000 students in a rural Midwestern town. She has traveled widely and frequently thus far this fall, and Jackie is looking forward to connecting with a high school guidance counselor friend, Alister, during her upcoming trip to several East Coast states.

Jackie and Alister met at a summer workshop for new admission professionals and hit it off immediately. The two women shared similar interests and activities as undergraduates, and both had gone immediately into college admissions work. While Jackie is working at her college alma mater as an admissions counselor, Alister is employed at her prep school alma mater, Lakeview Academy, as a college counselor. Alister helps students and their parents make plans for college and navigate the increasingly complex admissions processes. Jackie visited Alister at her Lakeview Academy office on a Friday morning, at the end of a long week of school visits and applicant interviews. She hoped that she and Alister could spend time together over the weekend, since she had never been to this city before and wanted to have some fun and relax.

The visit to Lakeview went quite well, with over a dozen students coming to meet with Jackie about Westergrove. Jackie suspected that her relationship with Alister may have boosted Westergrove's popularity among the senior class, but she was nonetheless pleased to meet with so many interested and high-quality prospective students. As Alister walked Jackie to her car, she invited her for drinks at a popular watering hole. Jackie accepted, and Alister agreed to pick up Jackie at 6 p.m.

After a few happy hour drinks and appetizers at the bar, Alister suggested that they get out of the smoke and noisy crowd and go to a party at the home of one of her fellow staff members from Lakeview. On the way over, Alister mentioned that the party could be large and that she was not exactly sure who would be there. Upon arrival, Jackie noted that many members of the Lakeview Academy's staff were there, as well as a number of people who Alister introduced as parents of Lakeview students.

As Alister introduced Jackie to parents, she added with a conspiratorial whisper, "She's the one who can get our students into Westergrove."

Jackie felt a bit uncomfortable but decided to laugh and treat the remark as a joke. Before long, Jackie found herself cornered in the kitchen by two well-meaning but aggressive parents who wanted her to give them the "inside scoop" on getting their children into selective colleges. They both added that they had been significant financial contributors to Lakeview and wanted to do the same for the colleges that their children will one day attend. One parent then said, "Alister tells me you're in town for the whole weekend. Will you and Alister be our guests at the country club tomorrow? You can swim or ride or just relax, and I'd love for you to meet my children over lunch, so you can get to know them better. One's a freshman and one's a sophomore at Lakeview."

What should Jackie do and why?

Magazine Article or Admission Essay?

Leah Ewing Ross
MGT of America, Inc.

Scenic College is one of four private liberal arts colleges located in a small city on the East Coast. The 900 students at Scenic represent 40 states and 50 countries, though most of the students come from the state in which Scenic is located and the contiguous states. Scenic is a tuition-driven institution, yet the admission program is selective and highly personalized. A great deal of attention is paid to applicants' admission essays and letters of recommendation, and a lot of emphasis is placed on diversifying the student body. The average SAT score is 1170; the average high school grade point average (GPA) is 3.5; and 75% of students graduated in the top 20% of their high school classes. Most of the students at Scenic are primarily focused on their academic experiences but are well-rounded and active on campus.

Sophia, an admission counselor in her second year of work at Scenic College, was reviewing an application for admission and found that the student's essay seemed familiar. She had never experienced a situation in which she doubted the authenticity of an applicant's work and asked John, a fellow admission counselor, for his opinion. John read a few lines and agreed that the content sounded familiar. Together, Sophia and John used an Internet search engine and found a web version of an article that had been recently published in a popular news magazine. The applicant, Helen, had presented a slightly altered version of the magazine article as her admission essay.

Helen lives in the same state in which Scenic College is located, and the Office of Admission had spent several years building rapport and a favorable reputation with the high school she attends. In fact, Sophia currently is the Office of Admission's liaison to this school. The high school is very diverse and is located in a poor socioeconomic area with a high population of immigrants. Helen is a bright student and serves as student council president. Her GPA, standardized test scores, and class rank are well above the average of students accepted at Scenic, and she has completed a rigorous high school curriculum. Helen will be a first-generation college student; English is her second language, and Sophia wondered whether Helen fully understood the college application process.

The Scenic College application form included a place for students to list other colleges to which they have applied for admission. Helen noted on her form that she had also applied for admission to State University, the flagship campus of the state university system. State University is a prestigious, highly selective institution. The Scenic admission staff and the State University admission staff are well connected; in fact, a friend of Sophia's is an admission counselor there. The Scenic staff knows that their counterparts in the admission office at State pay little attention to essays in the University's admission process. They are confident that Helen will be admitted to State University in light of her academic record and standardized test scores. Furthermore, she is a desirable candidate for admission, because she will help to diversify State's student body.

Sophia requested a meeting with Catherine, director of the Scenic Office of Admission, to tell her about the situation. After listening to Sophia's description of the situation, Catherine asked Sophia to call Helen and ask for clarification. Sophia reached Helen, identified herself, and said, "Helen, we have been reviewing your application and have a question about your admission essay."

Before Sophia proceeded further, Helen interrupted with, "I need to tell you that I have decided to withdraw my application for admission to Scenic College," and then hung up.

What should Sophia do and why?

Exceptions in Graduate Admissions

Monica Parikh
University at Buffalo

Jamie recently began an admissions position just after graduating with his master's degree. He, his five fellow assistant directors, and the Director of Graduate Admissions facilitate the application process for 32 graduate programs at Legacy University, a private, highly selective research university. Legacy recently created this graduate admissions office, removing significant administrative burdens from the faculty in the individual programs. The Graduate Admissions Office receives all materials from students who have applied for graduate admission and maintains contact with applicants regarding the status of their applications.

The office is relatively small, but the staff members all strive to be responsive and efficient with their services. Jamie and the other assistant directors perform many tasks: they communicate with students who are interested in the programs, convey different programs' requirements, attend graduate college fairs (sometimes with and sometimes without faculty representatives), and encourage students to apply. Assistant directors also follow up with applicants to ensure that applications are completed by the appropriate deadline. As deadlines approach, assistant directors also inform prospective students via e-mail of any items needed to complete the application. Completed applications are forwarded to the academic department for review, and applicants receive e-mails confirming that the application has been forwarded and that a decision will be forthcoming.

Two weeks before one program's application deadline, Jamie reviewed his list of in-process applicants and e-mailed one student who applied to this particular program:

Dear Mr. Grandview,

Thank you for your application. However, it is incomplete. We have received all materials except your GRE scores. They are required for admission to this program, and we cannot complete your application until the official scores arrive. Please understand that the admission deadline for this program is two weeks from today.

Please let me know if you have any questions.

Thank you.

Applicant Grandview quickly responded:

Thank you for the e-mail. But I was told I don't have to take the GRE. I met with Professor Basil a few weeks ago, who specifically said that I wouldn't need the scores. Dr. Basil used the term "waive"—he said they would be waived, because I did so well in my master's degree, which also didn't require GRE scores for admission. At Dr. Basil's request, I forwarded copies of all my other admission materials directly to him, since he told me that was all they would need to make a decision.

Can you get back to me as soon as possible about this?

Jamie wondered if the student was trying to get away with something. Jamie asked two of his assistant director colleagues and learned that they had had similar e-mail and phone communications with a few other applicants. Jamie was concerned, because the uniform GRE requirement, along with all other changes in graduate admission processes, was adopted and endorsed by an advisory committee of Legacy University faculty prior to the creation of the graduate admissions office.

What should Jamie do and why?

Commencement Ethics

Gypsy Denzine
Northern Arizona University

After a rash of resignations and retirements among senior staff members, Tyrone has recently been appointed interim assistant dean of student services in the large College of Arts and Sciences at East Coast Polytechnic University (ECPU), a public research institution with an enrollment of 35,000 undergraduate students in a major metropolitan area. Tyrone had served for three years as academic advisor in the college. One of Tyrone's responsibilities as the assistant dean is to plan commencement for the college. Tomorrow is spring commencement, so today is a busy day for Tyrone and for his colleagues in the Dean's Office, most of whom are busy with parent-, alumni-, or commencement-related activities that are also being held today. However, when Tyrone heard that a parent wanted to meet with him this morning, he made time for the meeting.

The parent, Mr. Nakano, had just arrived from Japan and came to see Tyrone because he had seen the printed program for commencement and was disappointed that his son Shawn's name did not appear in the list of graduates. In the Arts and Sciences College, commencement brochures were printed two weeks in advance so that students could mail these brochures to their families prior to the ceremony. Mr. Nakano said, "Shawn told us that his name hadn't been included because of an administrative error but can't that be corrected? This is a big event in our son's life and in ours, too. We want to be able to show this to our family back home, so they can share Shawn's achievement as well."

Tyrone, recalling how he had checked and double-checked the graduates' names against university records, replied, "I do understand your disappointment, but we can't print revised brochures at this late date." Mr. Nakano then asked if an erratum could be published. When Tyrone answered that he was not sure if printing an erratum or insert would be possible, Mr. Nakano replied that he would come back to Tyrone's office at the end of the day in case he could pick up some formal errata sheets or inserts that could be distributed to family members in Japan.

After Mr. Nakano left the office, Tyrone looked up the student's academic records. According to Shawn's academic transcript, Shawn changed his major several times during his first year at ECPU and failed all of his courses during the fall semester of his second year. There was no record of Shawn's enrollment since that time. Tyrone looked up Shawn's name in the local phone book and saw that he was living in town. He called the number, asked to speak with Shawn, and was told, "Shawn's at work. Let me give you his cell phone number."

Tyrone left a message on Shawn's cell phone asking Shawn to call him later that day. When Shawn returned Tyrone's call, Tyrone asked Shawn about his academic status at ECPU. Shawn sighed and said, "Has my father contacted you?"

When Tyrone confirmed this, Shawn admitted that he dropped out of college at the beginning of his second year. He asked Tyrone not to say anything to his father, because his family has been sending him money for tuition, housing, and all college expenses for the past four years. Shawn did not want to disappoint his family, so he did not tell them he was not graduating tomorrow.

When Tyrone pressed him, Shawn admitted that he planned to "walk" at commencement tomorrow. However, he would not tell Tyrone which one of the five ECPU colleges' commencement activities he planned to participate in.

At ECPU, each student who met graduation requirements would be issued a card with his or her name on it, which the student handed to the reader prior to crossing the stage. As graduates crossed the stage, they shook the president's hand and received a scroll with a generic message of congratulations. Actual degrees would be mailed after the final degree audit and transcript review was conducted by the registrar's office. Shawn has a friend who decided not to participate in graduation and has given Shawn his card to use. "But the reader won't be saying your name," interrupted Tyrone.

Shawn said, "Yes, but I'll just tell my parents that the reader made a mistake and read the wrong name."

Tyrone shared his concerns and encouraged Shawn to reconsider his decision to misrepresent his graduation to his family. Shawn explained that he has a good job and has no plans to return to Japan permanently, so his family will never know that he did not graduate. Tyrone then told Shawn that he has a responsibility to uphold the academic integrity of commencement and asked Shawn not to falsely participate in the ceremony tomorrow. Shawn replied, "Thousands of students are graduating tomorrow, and one more student won't hurt anyone. Besides, don't you see that I'm doing this for my parents?"

What should Tyrone do and why?

5

Residence Life Cases

Building Dedication and Pool Table

Craig Chatriand and Michelle Boettcher
Iowa State University

Brad just graduated with his master's degree in educational leadership and is a first-year hall director in Clark Hall, the newest building on the campus of Midwest State University. His hall houses 350 mostly first-year students with a small number of upper division students. The building also includes classroom space. This particular semester, a social justice course made up of mostly third-year sociology majors is being taught in the building. One of the assignments for the class is called "Action on Injustice;" students must identify a social problem on campus or in the community and develop and implement a project for academic credit to highlight and address the issue. Approximately 5 of the 20 students enrolled in this social justice class are also residents of the building.

Clark Hall was recently named after individuals in the community, now deceased, who were instrumental in boarding students before on-campus housing was available to all Midwest State University students. Specifically, this local family housed and fed African American students for a number of years from the

1920s until after World War II because of discriminatory housing practices in the community and on campus. When the number of African American students grew to a point where the Clark family could not house them all, Davis Clark met with the president of Midwest State University and worked to end the discriminatory campus housing practices that targeted African American students.

The Clark family and the work they did for African American students was highlighted on campus as part of the naming ceremony activities for Clark Hall, and the Clarks have been discussed several times in the social justice class as an example of how one person, or in this case one family, can make a difference. The five students taking the course and living in the building have expressed interest as a group in talking with descendents from the Clark family to learn more about the family for whom their building is named.

These same five students live on one floor of the building and want to petition their floor council to buy a pool table for its lounge with money from the floor government. Many of the residence hall floors across campus have pool tables, video games, ping-pong tables, and so forth to help facilitate community among the residents. Brad explained to them the process involved in petitioning for this purchase and sent them on their way.

A few days later, Brad received a call from the granddaughter of the family for whom the building was named complaining that she heard that a pool table was going to be housed in the building that bears her grandparents' name. She said, "Brad, my grandmother was violently opposed to gambling and to the 'pool hall culture.' She would be horrified to have her name associated with that type of activity." The granddaughter, who Brad had met at the dedication ceremony, asked what she could do to stop this from happening.

At the same time, Susan, the professor who is teaching the social justice class, stopped by Brad's office to visit and mentioned to him that the group of five students was planning to meet with descendents of the family. The students wanted to explore how the family members felt issues for students had evolved and what challenges remain, as a precursor to identifying potential "Action on Injustice" topics or projects that they could pursue. Susan added, "Isn't that a great idea?"

What should Brad do and why?

The Partying, On-duty RA

McCarren Caputa
University of Puget Sound

W. Houston Dougharty
Lewis and Clark College

As a resident director (RD) at a medium-size, public, comprehensive institution, Nick is responsible for supervising 15 resident assistants (RAs) who live and work in two adjacent residence halls. The year has gone very smoothly, especially for Nick's first year out of graduate school and on the job. He feels good about the staff that he inherited—they have jelled into a great team, and the residents seem to respect them and respond positively to their role modeling and programming. Nick is particularly proud of the four RAs who are just sophomores.

After a mid-spring semester staff meeting, Jessica, one of these sophomore RAs, approached Nick sheepishly and asked to have a private conversation about something serious. Nick was concerned and quite curious about this and invited Jessica down the hall into his office. She followed him closely and asked that he close the door.

Jessica, who was usually vivacious and quite talkative, sat somberly on the couch, obviously very disturbed and worried. She slowly, quietly shared, "I feel terrible about this, but there's something I've needed to tell you for a few weeks now, and I just can't keep it to myself anymore."

After a long pause, Nick responded, "Jessica, I want you to be up-front and honest, and I want to be supportive of you."

Still quite reluctant and nervous, she began to tell Nick her concern about Stephanie, a fellow sophomore RA in the other residence hall. Jessica told Nick, "A few weeks ago, I was at a frat party with my friend Leah. I saw Stephanie there. She was trashed. I couldn't believe how much beer she drank. We didn't get there until 9, and one of the guys in the house said she'd been there since 7 and was doing shots with some of the brothers and drinking beer the whole time. I was really worried about her. I didn't realize it at the time, but later I found out that some of our residents were at the party, too, and they saw her. Since that party, some of the residents have been arguing with me and other RAs when they're confronted about violating the residence life alcohol policy. They've been saying stuff about Stephanie, like 'Why is it okay for one of the RAs to be out drinking underage, and we get busted for it?' One of the other RAs asked what they were talking about, and they said, 'You ask her if she had fun at the Beta Tau house the other day. She didn't seem to have any problems with drinking there.'"

Jessica went on to tell Nick that not only was Stephanie (who is underage at 20 years old) drinking at the campus fraternity party, but that she may have been the on-call RA at the time—at least according to what she said at the party. The on-call RA, who serves as the emergency contact and point person for her residence hall that entire evening, must be in the residence hall while on-call and is responsible for documenting any safety concerns or policy violations during her on-call shift, which is typically 8 p.m. to 8 a.m. According to Jessica, as Stephanie drank more at the party, she began to boldly announce, "Hey, being on-call isn't so bad!"

After Nick listened to all that Jessica unloaded, he thanked her for being willing to talk with him about this. Nick then told her that he would explore this further with Stephanie. Jessica immediately panicked. "You can't tell her where you heard about this, Nick. I'm serious. Please don't tell her. She's a good friend, and if she knows that I told you, it'll ruin our friendship, and we'll never be able to work together. Promise me that you won't tell her."

What should Nick do and why?

Exercise of Religion Among Student Staff

Craig Chatriand and Michelle Boettcher
Iowa State University

Dana is a first-year, full-time, hall director at Monumental University, a small, public historically Black university in the Southeast. When MU opens this fall, he will manage two residence halls and supervise 15 resident assistants (RAs). One of Dana's buildings is Groten Hall, which has a staff of seven RAs including three new RAs who were hired just last spring. Dana reports to Jim, the Director of Housing at MU. Over the summer, Dana e-mailed his student staff members to let them know who he is and to share a little about himself. He received welcoming and upbeat responses from all seven RAs.

In her reply e-mail to Dana, Rhonda, who will be a first-year Groten RA, expressed her enthusiasm about the position. She wrote about her travels during the summer and excitement about returning to campus and being an RA. She also offered to coordinate some welcome week activities for new students in the building, since "it was so helpful to me when I was a freshman to make contact with people I could feel comfortable with." At the end of her e-mail on the signature line was the passage "May you be blessed by the Lord who made heaven and earth!"

Dana asked Lynn, a second-year hall director, what the policy was regarding student staff and religion on campus, and Lynn explained, "As long as it doesn't interfere with their ability to connect with students, it's fine. Actually, it may make them more approachable to a number of MU students." Lynn also showed Dana a copy of the student staff expectations, which included the provision, "Every staff member must be available, accessible, and approachable to residents." Dana reread the rest of the document and could not find any other sections that seemed relevant to this situation.

Dana asked Jim about the situation and was told that, since the department does not furnish the university e-mail account, he cannot mandate what his staff members put or do not put in their e-mail messages. In this case, Jim said as long as the student staff member does not note that she is an RA in the title line of her signature, the passage is acceptable.

When Rhonda arrived on campus on a Saturday in mid-August, she was friendly and enthusiastic as she met Dana. She reiterated her interest in working with students during welcome week and shared some fliers she created for potential programs.

While Dana was walking around meeting and greeting the staff on Saturday, he saw that Rhonda had posted a number of scriptures on her door, and she displayed three crosses in her room on the wall and on her dresser. She had also posted a flier next to her door advertising an event during welcome week hosted by ABC, All

Blessed in Christ, a student religious organization on campus. Because Dana was unsure of whether this was acceptable freedom of speech or improper promotion of religion, he scheduled a meeting with Jim for the first break in the training schedule on Monday.

Ray, one of the returning Groten RAs, came to Dana on the Sunday afternoon of opening weekend. Ray said that two of Rhonda's residents had approached him, because they felt that Rhonda had pressured them to go to church with her that morning. Ray also said that Rhonda was now posting signs for a welcome week Bible study and BBQ and said she had gotten Dana's approval. As he walked through the building, Dana saw a number of bright orange signs that read "Welcome Week Christian Cook-Out: Bring your Bibles; we'll bring burgers."

What should Dana do and why?

The 21st Birthday Party

Deborah J. Taub
University of North Carolina-Greensboro

Jennifer, age 24, has just started her first professional student affairs position after graduate school. She is a Community Residence Director at Middle State University (MSU). Middle State is a campus of about 14,000 students, located in a predominantly rural portion of a Midwestern state. The town in which the campus is situated is approximately 90 minutes from the closest sizeable urban area, which also is the location of the closest shopping mall. Immediately adjacent to the attractive Middle State campus are an assortment of fast-food restaurants and pizza places, a book store, a drug/discount store, and a number of bars typically frequented by MSU students. In her position, Jennifer supervises a staff of 12 undergraduate paraprofessionals. Despite her concerns about being in her first supervisory position, in the few weeks that she has been on the job, she feels that she has established a growing rapport with the staff. Student staff training has just wrapped up, and it has gone well.

Not everything was going well, however. Jennifer's orientation to her new position had been rather cursory, and she received much less formal training than she would have expected.

"It's more a learn-on-the-job type of thing," explained her hurried supervisor Greg. Jennifer had important business office paperwork and procedures explained to her; she'd been shown the basics of her job; and she was thrown into the already planned student staff training. However, she hadn't really been acquainted with specific department or university policies.

Jennifer also was lonely at Middle State. She missed the tight-knit group of students she was part of in graduate school. Although she had exchanged e-mails with her friends, everyone has seemed busy and wrapped up in their transitions to their new positions. It also seemed to Jennifer that they were all doing much better than her; they certainly seemed happy and confident, and she grew aware of her feelings of envy. She had been reluctant to share her doubts and concerns with them. To Jennifer's surprise, much of the MSU residence life staff was older than her (even if only by a few years) and married or with partners. Jennifer was the only new Community Residence Director this year. Although other staff members made attempts to reach out to her, Jennifer felt that they were at different stages of life than she was and suspected that they were merely being kind. She had little chance to meet many staff members beyond residence life yet, since she had been so involved in staff training. Jennifer found herself looking forward to her interactions with her young and lively student staff members, with whom she felt she had much in common.

A group of four of her student staff members dropped by Jennifer's office to mention that today was Mike's 21st birthday (Mike is on the RA staff). They invited her to join them for the celebration, saying, "We stopped by to see if you want to come with us for Mike's birthday celebration tonight. We're meeting in his room at 9 to go to Dino's."

Jennifer recognized the location as a well-known bar just off campus, frequented by undergraduates. Without giving it much thought, Jennifer responded as they rushed off, "Wow! Thanks!"

Jennifer found herself smiling. She was flattered that her staff had offered to include her; she really wanted them to like her. And, a night out certainly sounded a lot better than staying in to watch TV, which was what she had planned for the evening. She recalled the sorts of evenings she spent with her graduate school buddies and felt those familiar pangs of loneliness and homesickness for graduate school again. She daydreamed for a few minutes and then returned to the stack of paperwork on her desk.

As members of the RA staff passed by her office door in the afternoon, they called out, "See you tonight!" The first time that happened, Jennifer remembered with a start the casual conversation that she had had earlier in the day about Mike's birthday party. She realized with pleasure that the invitation had been genuine.

"It would be an opportunity to bond with the staff," Jennifer mused to herself. "And, it's Mike's 21st birthday; things could get a little wild. Maybe I'd be a good influence on them and keep them safe."

What should Jennifer do and why?

Hiring a Diverse Staff

Michelle Boettcher and Craig Chatriand
Iowa State University

Marcus is a hall director at Southwest State University, a small (2,500-student), public baccalaureate university. The Office of Residence Life houses approximately 700 students, mostly first years, in three different residence halls. This is Marcus's second year working for the Office of Residence Life and his first year serving on the Resident Assistant Selection Committee. Of the 20 resident assistants employed by the department, 13 are planning to return next year, so the committee must fill seven positions. To be eligible for an RA position, one must be a full time student of at least sophomore status and have a GPA of 2.5 or higher. Candidates are also informed via the position announcement that being an RA involves effective leadership, teamwork, and communication. Cheryl, the Assistant Director for Residence Life who serves as RA Selection Committee chair, provided the list of these criteria at the initial meeting to the committee members, who are Marcus and the directors of the other two halls.

The Resident Assistant Selection Committee received 19 completed applications for the seven open positions. All 19 candidates went through group interviews and individual interviews conducted by the three hall directors and a group of current RAs and were subsequently ranked based on performance in areas such as teamwork, leadership skills, and confrontation skills. At the next committee meeting, Cheryl asked the committee members to identify candidates' race and ethnicity based on observable features and/or names. Five of the nineteen candidates were identified as students of color. Two of these five candidates had been ranked within the top five, while the remaining three students had scored in the bottom ten to fifteen.

Cheryl said, "Thanks very much for all of your hard work with the interviewing phase. As you know, the interviews and rankings are one part of the selection process, and we will be offering RA positions to all five of the students of color. Our remaining task is to recommend two additional candidates to fill the other two slots. And of course, I'd like you to identify some top alternates in case any of these seven turn down our offers. So, who are your top picks from the rest of the pool?"

As Cheryl spoke, Marcus looked again at his notes and recalled some serious concerns that were voiced by participating RAs about all of the students that were ranked in the bottom ten. The comments had included concerns about abilities to foster relationships, relative degrees of tolerance for religious beliefs or sexual orientation, and abilities to confront negative behaviors. During one of the interview debriefing sessions with his participating RAs, one of them said, "Oh, you really can't hire this person. I don't have any confidence that she would take the job seriously." Marcus remembered that this comment was made in reference to one of the three students who had been ranked very low in the candidate pool.

Marcus also remembered that he shared many of these same concerns about candidates during the interview processes, and he did not recall any committee discussions prior to this about ensuring staff diversity or ways to recruit students of color to the RA candidate pool. Marcus did a quick count and concluded that, of the 13 returning RAs, one was African American and two were Native Americans.

What should Marcus do and why?

Supervision, Accountability, and Confidentiality

Ryan J. Davis
University of Maryland, College Park

Camille Mills College (CMC) is a medium-size, private, liberal arts institution in northeastern Connecticut. CMC's total student enrollment is 5,400 with an on-campus population of 2,200. The Department of Housing and Residential Life is staffed by a director, one associate director, three area coordinators, seven full-time hall directors (HDs) and 65 resident assistants (RAs).

David held a graduate assistantship in the Office of Greek Life at CMC for the past two years while he was completing his master's degree in college personnel administration at a nearby university. Prior to his graduation three months ago, David sought different kinds of experiences in student affairs for his first professional position. As part of his job search, he had applied and was hired as a HD at CMC. He is satisfied with his decision for many reasons, including the fact that he was already quite familiar with CMC from his assistantship experience. As a direct result of his assistantship work, David already has established many key relationships across campus.

Candice is a sophomore and a new RA on David's staff. She has a vibrant personality, great energy, charisma, and innovative programming ideas. However, Candice struggles to complete her RA administrative duties in a timely manner and continuously rushes her weekly one-on-one supervision meetings with David. Additionally, Candice missed one RA staff meeting in late September with an inexcusable explanation: "It just slipped my mind." Shortly after this incident during her most recent one-on-one meeting with David, Candice confided that she was not doing well in classes and had to ask her instructors for extensions on some of her course assignments. David voiced his concerns about her work performance and her academics, noting that RAs were required to maintain a minimum 2.50 GPA in order to keep their positions. He also placed documentation of their conversations in her file. When David asked Candice how he could help her, Candice replied, "Thanks, but I'll figure it out. It takes me a little while to get started and balance everything out. I just need to work out some time management stuff, and I'll be fine." After this meeting and their follow-up discussion in early October, David was confident that Candice's performance would improve. It is now mid-October, and David feels he has given Candice ample time to adjust to her position as an RA.

The date was October 18th, and the next RA staff meeting was scheduled for that evening. At 2:45 p.m., David retrieved a message on his voicemail from Candice. David guessed that Candice dialed his direct voice message extension because the recorded time of the message was 2:30 pm, and David had not left his office between 1:30 and 3:00 nor did he hear the phone ring during this time. On the message, Candice told David, "I'm really sorry, but I'm going to have to miss the staff meeting tonight. I have class. I'll catch up with you or one of the other RAs and get all the information." As David was listening to the message, he reminded himself that his staff members' classes do not conflict with any scheduled meetings for the semester; he had collected their class schedules before arranging the final staff meeting schedule after the undergraduate add/drop deadline. David attempted unsuccessfully to reach Candice via her room phone and cell phone to discuss the situation with her. He left messages asking her to meet with him the following afternoon. Since David began his position as a HD, he had not had to confront staff members about issues surrounding job performance, with the exception of Candice's initial dilemma with time management. He also knew Candice's second absence from a staff meeting wouldn't escape her fellow RAs' attention.

When David met with Candice the following afternoon, she reported that she had to attend a course requirement of ART 101: Introduction to Theater Arts. She then clarified that the class meets on Monday, Wednesday, and Friday at 10:00 a.m., but one of the required assignments is to attend two of six different university theater performances during the semester and write a one-page paper. When David asked Candice the name of the performance she attended, Candice looked startled, and after a moment admitted that she had not attended a performance but instead had to reserve this space in her schedule to pledge into the same National Pan-Hellenic Council (NPHC) sorority with which her mother is also affiliated. She apologized profusely for missing the staff meeting, but insisted that David and she not discuss her sorority involvement any further because she had to keep going "on-line" until December. David recognized this as an unofficial term, not promoted by NPHC, which refers to the Membership Intake Process. Because of his previous employment in the Office of Greek Life and affiliation with a NPHC fraternity, David knew that going "on-line," at least as it had been practiced among CMC chapters, involved illegal hazing activities and was prohibited by both CMC and NPHC policies.

What should David do and why?

Thursday at Copoa

Donavan McCargo
Rowan University

Copoa University is a predominantly White, four-year, private, comprehensive, liberal arts institution in the Northwestern United States. Copoa enrolls approximately 1,500 students (80% are White/Caucasian, and 400 are first-year students). Approximately 1,000 students live on campus. Toward the end of fall semester, a few members of Black Students United (BSU) and a popular White fraternity named Alpha Pi were involved in a scuffle during their championship intramural basketball game. As a result of this altercation, the dean of students issued one year suspensions from intramural participation to two members of BSU who were accused of starting the fight and placed three members of Alpha Pi on probation for two semesters.

However, the situation remained controversial at CU. Early the following spring semester, one student who identified himself as African American and an eyewitness to the fight wrote in a letter published in the campus newspaper, "I saw it. The Alpha Pi guy threw the first punch. But what does that get you on this campus? I'm guessing that Alpha Pi's advisor is friends with the dean, and the dean must have cut his guys some slack."

CU's Greek letter organizations do not have houses, and several members of both BSU and Alpha Pi live in Keen, a popular CU residence hall. The residence life staff members suspected that tensions would continue to run high during spring semester. Kyle, Keen's first-year hall director and BSU's advisor, decided to meet with members of BSU the next morning to see if they could identify a positive plan of action for resolving the tension between the two organizations. Kris, the vice president of Alpha Pi who is also a community advisor in Keen, requested a meeting later in the week with Kyle to offer his help. Kyle had become somewhat irritated with the situation and had privately wondered about the fairness of the sanctions that the students involved in the fight had received.

As Kyle approached his office the following morning to meet with BSU members, he noticed that the creative expression bulletin board had a new poster with the words "die monkeys die" scrawled underneath a crude drawing of a bandaged and bruised monkey sporting an Afro. A group of students stood near the poster, whispering and pointing. One took a photo of the poster with her cell phone. Kyle quickly removed the poster and continued to his office where he placed it face down behind his desk.

He found that the BSU members waiting at his office had already seen the poster, and they were outraged. One of the BSU's officers quietly remarked, "You know, if someone can make a bad cartoon of a beating, and one beating has already happened on this campus, what's next? I'm going to lock my door, look over my shoulder, and not go around alone." The other members nodded their agreement, some angrily, some quietly.

Kyle decided to visit with his colleague and friend Jay about the situation. Jay is a second-year hall director of Lake Hall and an alumni advisor to Alpha Pi. As Kyle walked toward Jay's apartment, Kyle saw Kris and Jay standing outside the apartment door. As Jay got closer, he heard their laughter and Kris's remark, "Yeah, and the poster's all over campus now thanks to cell phones and e-mail."

Jay turned to see Kyle approaching and quickly told Kris that he would catch up with him later. As Kris passed by, Kyle smelled alcohol. Although he was angry and upset, Kyle asked Jay if they could visit at a later time. On Kyle's walk home he thought, "Just a week ago, I wrote a letter on Jay's behalf to a student affairs recognition committee. He's up for an award honoring his commitment to students and his high ethical standards. What was I thinking?"

When Kyle arrived at his office the following morning, he retrieved two voicemails. The first was from the Dean of Students Office to inform Kyle that his community advisor Kris and another Keen resident had been arrested by the local police for public intoxication and creating a disturbance and to ask Kyle to call the dean's office as soon as possible. The second voicemail message was from Jay, who said, "Kyle, I need to talk to you right away. Call me as soon as you get this message."

What should Kyle do and why?

An Arresting RA Development

McCarren Caputa
University of Puget Sound

W. Houston Dougharty
Lewis and Clark College

Parker is a live-in, second-year resident director (RD) at a small, private, urban baccalaureate college in New England, responsible for supervising a five-person resident assistant (RA) staff in a coed residence hall. Sarah, a third-year RA and a senior on Parker's staff, called him at home late one Thursday evening. While he was used to getting calls late at night, it was rare for Sarah to need much assistance, since she is a third-year staff member, has great skills and confidence, and establishes strong connections with her residents and the other staff in the hall.

After Sarah apologized for bothering Parker at home, she asked if he has permanent home phone numbers for residents in the hall. While Parker had access to this information, he knew that he was not supposed to give it to student staff members.

Parker asked, "Why do you need these numbers, Sarah?"

Sarah replied, "I really can't explain it right now. I just really need the phone numbers, Parker."

After a few awkward attempts to get the number from him, Sarah gave up, apologized again for bothering him, and hung up. However, after a moment or two, Parker grew increasingly suspicious about Sarah's motives and called her room, but there was no answer. Parker left her a message, asking her to touch base with him the next day. He also called her cell phone and left the same message. Parker hopped on the computer to see if she was available by instant message, but she wasn't. Her away message said, "Helping folks." While he was concerned about the situation, he trusted her judgment and made a note to find her the next morning to see what's up.

By noon Friday, Parker had yet to see Sarah. That was unusual, because they often ran into each other at breakfast or at the café. He left a message on her door, asking her to check in at her earliest convenience.

Around 3:00 p.m., as the hall was filling with the energy of weekend activity, Parker looked up from his desk and saw Sarah standing in his office doorway. She launched into another apology for bothering him last night. Parker quickly replied, "You're always welcome to call me. Please go ahead and have a seat. Did you get the messages I left for you?"

After Sarah nodded, Parker asked, "So, what was that all about, anyway?"

Sarah, not too eagerly, told him that two of her first-year residents were arrested for shoplifting at a nearby mall yesterday. They told Sarah that they didn't want the school or their parents to get involved and were "trying to just handle it themselves." They had called Sarah from the police station, hoping that she could bail them out. After hanging up with the residents, Sarah felt like she needed to contact their parents anyway. When she couldn't get parent information from Parker—and she understood that he couldn't release it—Sarah and the roommates of the arrested women went through their rooms looking for home phone numbers, hoping to contact family members for bail money and to let them know what was going on.

They found the phone numbers, contacted the parents, and arranged for the women to post bail. The women were back on campus awaiting their parents' arrival for the impending court dates. Sarah said she really hoped that Parker would keep all this information to himself so that the college will not send the women through the conduct system. "Because you know," she said, "they're really great girls, and they didn't do anything wrong on campus."

Parker reminded her that the campus honor code pertains to "all behavior violating the honor code," whether on or off campus. During their conversation, Parker was conscious of making a mental list of people to contact, and he started to think about how he could be helpful as a supervisor to Sarah. Sarah looked down at her lap and said quietly, "But I told the girls that I would help them keep this quiet."

What should Parker do and why?

The Rumor Mill

Jayme Uden
University of Kansas

Kipp Van Dyke and Camilla Jones
Kansas State University

Carter is a hall director at Skye State University (SSU), a midsize comprehensive university on the West Coast. SSU's housing department employs eight other hall directors. Each hall director supervises one graduate assistant, a staff of anywhere from 10 to 15 resident assistants (RAs), and numerous desk workers. The hall directors and graduate assistants make up a team of 18 individuals that are known as the senior staff. The senior staff has functioned effectively and productively for the most part during the last several years, collaborating on programming efforts, training sessions, and other tasks.

Carter enjoyed getting to know Maggie, the graduate student he supervises, and the two of them began to develop an effective working relationship as well as a strong friendship. Carter was worried, though, about some of the relationships that Maggie had formed with a few of the other senior staff members. She was especially close to a graduate assistant in another hall, Michael, and two hall directors, Michelle and Matt. They spent a lot of time together, and the senior staff had informally dubbed them the "Mod Squad."

From talking to Maggie, Carter knew that the Mod Squad often vented to each other electronically and in person about work issues, which Maggie appreciated as a release. They occasionally would discuss their impressions of senior staff members. Carter also learned from Maggie that a few RAs and desk workers who work for Michelle or Matt have also been part of the discussions about senior staff members. During breakfast in the dining hall one morning, Maggie asked Carter about a few of the rumors surrounding other hall directors, specifically one about Renee, Michael's direct supervisor. "From what I hear, Renee isn't going to get the prize for working the most hours. Did you know that she only works about three hours a day? I wish I could figure out how that works!"

Carter seriously doubted this because he had been impressed with how smoothly Renee's building was run, but Maggie told him that a lot of students and senior staff members were talking about it.

Carter had been at lunch a few times with some of the Mod Squad at one of the campus dining halls, and he also noticed that there were often some RAs present who contributed to the gossip. Carter managed to change the topic of conversation multiple times to something more appropriate but had yet to confront anyone directly.

One day at a senior staff meeting, Rick, the assistant director of Residence Life, spoke of concerns he had about his perceptions of divisiveness among staff members, and asked if something's going on. Renee responded, her voice shaking, "I wasn't going to bring this up in a meeting, but I guess if we're really a team, then this is the right place. I don't appreciate the rumors that have been spread about my work ethic and commitment. I work hard to make my hall a great place for students, and these rumors are ruining my reputation with my student staff and residents. I don't know where this stuff is coming from; I just want to know how to make it stop. If someone has issues with me, I need them to talk to me about it, not to everyone else."

Other senior staff members expressed concerns about work relationships and teamwork as well, but Carter noticed that Michelle, Matt, Michael, and Maggie remained silent during this discussion.

What should Carter do and why?

Who Is Living Here?

W. Houston Dougharty
Lewis and Clark College

Balancing the demands of life as a first-year, full-time graduate student and resident coordinator in family housing at the Principal State University's campus at San Tomas (a regional Hispanic-serving university enrolling 17,000 students in the western United States.) is no easy task, but Adrian thoroughly enjoys her position. Having a partner who works full-time at a local bank and a very active two-year-old toddler also makes her life very full.

One of the things Adrian likes best about her job is the wide variety of residents with whom she works—PSU students, mostly graduate students, and their families from several countries. The four apartment buildings that Adrian oversees house people of a variety of ages and life experiences who speak many different languages and study a variety of academic disciplines. She has gotten to know many of her residents well, and she regards many of them as friends and close neighbors.

PSU's family housing apartments are in high demand, and the university maintains clear eligibility requirements for residents. At least one resident must be a full-time PSU student, and they may reside with legally recognized partners or spouses and/or up to four children for whom the PSU student is legal guardian. Furthermore, the policy specifies that residents who violate this policy are subject to eviction. So far, only minor issues have arisen with family housing residents, and Adrian has realized that most of the problems have resulted from misunderstandings or misinterpretation of PSU policies.

Bernardo Gabaldon is a chemistry graduate student from Central America. He shares his apartment with his spouse, Margarita, and their two elementary-school-aged children, Inez and Luis. Both Bernando and Margarita are very active in the apartment complex and the university community. They have volunteered for many committees, participated in social events, and offered to watch other residents' children on occasion. Recently, they coordinated a program where they spoke about the current political and economic strife in their home country, and the difficulties faced by citizens there—including many of their own family members and friends back home. Bernardo added that he was an active member of the political opposition as a college student before coming to PSU for graduate work. He said, "Sometimes we fear for the safety of our relatives. I don't think we should return until the current ruling party is out of power."

Adrian's next door neighbor's seven-year-old son, Drew, often played with the Gabaldon children and spent a great deal of time at their apartment. One evening, Adrian and her partner invited Drew and his mom Kimberly over for a barbecue. In the middle of dinner, as they were talking about the larger than usual numbers of people in some of the apartment buildings this year, Drew added to his mom, "Yeah, and there are new people at Inez and Luis's house to play with now, too."

Adrian smiled and thought nothing of it, assuming he was referring to other children living in the complex. However, after dinner, Drew and Adrian's partner and their two-year old went into the living room to watch a video. Once they had left the kitchen, Kimberly told Adrian quietly, "There are rumors in the complex that there are nonstudents living at the Gabaldons' apartment, Adrian—people who only leave the apartment after dark." Kimberly added that neighbors think they are relatives who are in the country illegally. Kimberly begged Adrian not to tell anyone, because "everyone loves Bernardo and Margarita, and we don't want to see anything happen to them."

Adrian ran into Bernardo around midnight in the community laundry room, where Bernardo was carrying two large stacks of folded clothes and also holding Luis's hand. Luis yawned deeply and rubbed his eyes. When Adrian commented on his heavy load, Bernardo replied, "Yes, our kids go through a lot of clothes." He hesitated and then added, "And we have company. Margarita and I have a couple of relatives staying with us temporarily. But it won't be long. Their documents should come through any day now, and they can move on." Bernardo hurried out the door, telling Luis that he will go to bed soon.

The next morning Adrian attended the monthly Graduate Student Services meeting, which included representatives from Residence Life, the International Students Office, Enrollment Services, and the Student Health Center. On a monthly basis, this group gathered to discuss student services issues related to the international student population at PSU. Before the meeting started, Ted, an International Students Office staff member, took a seat beside Adrian. After saying hello, Ted said to Adrian, "I've been notified that there may be a problem with Bernardo Gabaldon's visa status. I need for you to send me verification of his residence at the student apartment complex—just an e-mail will be fine for now. And could you let him know that he should contact me ASAP? He hasn't responded to my phone messages or e-mails from yesterday. Have you seen him lately?"

What should Adrian do and why?

The Case of Karrie

Michael Dannells
Bowling Green State University

Kevin is the Director of Residence Life at Steffens College, a private, historically Black college that enrolls about 1,800 students in the small rural town of Steffens. Since finishing his master's degree program in college student personnel, Kevin has worked at Steffens for five years, serving as the assistant director of housing before he was promoted to director last year. He's very comfortable at Steffens and committed to its success. Kevin is also confident that, with last year's arrival of a new senior business officer and a new development director, Steffens is on the path to a much stronger financial footing as an institution. Kevin and his staff have also worked hard to develop the residence life program into an educational—and profitable—aspect of campus life. Affordable housing in the surrounding area is scarce, and the demand for campus housing is great.

Today, four days before the halls open for fall term, all of the residence halls are full and every room has been assigned. Additionally, 56 housing applicants remained on a waiting list for housing cancellations. Kevin reviewed this waiting list along with a list of temporary facilities and an inventory of furnishings. As he was considering temporary housing options, Kevin received a call from Dr. Joseph Guss, special assistant to the president, who informed Kevin that the president had a special circumstance that would require his immediate and confidential attention. Dr. Guss explained that a newly admitted (as of this morning) student, Karrie, required campus housing. Although Karrie had not applied for housing, her father made a direct appeal to the president, asking her to see that Karrie is assigned to Allen Hall where her mother had had such a wonderful experience as a Steffens student 25 years ago. The president wouldn't ordinarily get involved in these kinds of issues, Guss assured Kevin, but this situation really was exceptional. Not only are Karrie's parents faithful alumni of the college, Karri's father is the vice president of a chemical company that has made substantial contributions in recent years to the chemistry department at Steffens.

Kevin explained to Guss that every bed in Allen Hall, the most popular women's hall, was assigned, and roommates had been given each other's names. To assign Karrie at this late date would entail reneging on a commitment to an Allen resident. Guss said the president knew that Kevin was a good problem solver and that he would surely appreciate the larger picture. Kevin tried to end the conversation with Guss by saying, "I need to think about this," but Guss had the last word, saying matter-of-factly, "We need you to do more than that—and quickly."

A few minutes after his phone conversation with Dr. Guss, as his mental wheels were spinning, Dr. Thomas Larson called Kevin. Dr. Larson is the chair of the chemistry department where Kevin's spouse works as an administrative assistant. He reiterated the president's request, and added, "Kevin, I know I can count on you."

Kevin said, "Of course I'll do what I can," and said goodbye.

Later the same day Kevin told Kim, Allen's Hall Director, to put Karrie in a temporary triple (that is, assign her as a third resident in a standard double room) and added that room number to the list of rooms requiring an extra set of furniture. Kim raised concerns about the students still on the waiting list, but she complied with Kevin's request. Kim e-mailed the two other first-year roommates to inform them of their new roommate and to share Karrie's contact information.

Early the next day Kevin took a call from Dr. Marjorie Hawes, the director of Steffens College's student health services. Dr. Hawes had just met with Karrie and her mother, and Dr. Hawes agreed with Karrie's mother that Karrie's medical history of severe allergies and environmental sensitivities warranted her immediate assignment to a single room. Single rooms were not ordinarily available in Allen Hall; they were available only to upper-class students in Wilson Hall, a newer residence hall that was filled last spring via a lottery.

What should Kevin do and why?

Boys Will Be Boys

Kara Helgeson, Rebecca Rogge, and Alanna Keenan
Louisiana State University

Autumn, who is African American, is in her second year as judicial coordinator for housing at Deep South University (DSU), a large, public research university that is best known for its long tradition of excellence in intercollegiate athletics. Autumn had been excited to get the offer, since the position announcement had listed a preference for three to five years' experience, while she had just graduated with her master's degree and had two years' of assistantship experience in judicial affairs and residence life. Autumn maintains the housing department's judicial system and is liaison to DSU's Judicial Affairs Office based in the Dean of Students Office. She investigates and initiates appropriate actions on all reported Student Conduct Code violations in the residence halls and apartments.

Autumn felt she had learned a great deal in her relatively quiet first year of routine cases; she also was grateful for the strong support of her supervisor, Rick, who is assistant director of housing. Rick is a graduate of DSU (undergraduate and master's degrees) and had worked as a hall director at DSU for four years before beginning his current position within a month of Autumn's arrival. Autumn enjoys attending some of DSU's sporting events, and Rick is an avid fan as well as a member of the athletic foundation's board.

Rick had been looking forward to DSU's basketball season ever since Andy, a nationally ranked recruit from Idaho, had enrolled at DSU. However, Andy sustained a bone fracture and severe damage to one foot in an automobile accident in early fall. Andy received a medical red-shirt for this season, but the head coach has assured fans that Andy will be ready to play next year. However, Rick said to Autumn that his friend Nate, a DSU assistant basketball coach for the past 15 years who coordinates student academic issues, told him privately that Andy's rehabilitation was proceeding much more slowly than expected. Trainers and medical consultants had begun to suspect that his injuries may be more serious. Nate was concerned about Andy's level of frustration with the slow, painful rehabilitation and his apparent inabilities to focus on academics, and he also wondered whether Andy would be able to play again at top form.

After Andy returned to campus in the middle of the fall semester following his hospital stay, he and his two roommates, who were also teammates, were moved to a first-floor campus apartment. The apartments are managed by Alicia, who is in her first year at DSU after completing her master's degree (and one additional year of full-time residence hall experience) at another university in the state. Alicia and Autumn are currently the only African American professional staff members in housing and have become friends. Rick enjoys teasing Alicia good-naturedly about the rivalry between DSU and Alicia's alma mater.

Since Andy's return, he was written up for three violations of the noise policy, which is considered a low-level infraction. In the first case, Andy was one of a number of students in an apartment that was reported to the staff for loud music. All of the students in the apartment were documented. The second time Andy was documented for a noise policy violation, he and his roommates were screaming loudly while watching a Monday night football game; their neighbors had asked them to quiet down multiple times before calling the staff member. In each of these cases, Andy did not respond to Autumn's notifications of meetings and judicial hearings. In accordance with conduct code provisions, hearings were conducted in his absence and, in two cases, warnings were issued. In the third case, since it involved an additional violation of the same policy, a letter of sanction was prepared for his university records and forwarded to the campus Judicial Affairs Office. Autumn later heard from her colleague at Judicial Affairs that Nate had initiated an appeal of the housing department's sanction on Andy's behalf. This colleague then told Autumn, "Well, I guess you can't blame Coach Nate. He's thinks that 'boys will be boys,' and he's just trying to keep Andy out of trouble. Coach Nate has come to several of our judicial hearings when they've involved basketball players. He says he wants to be sure they aren't treated more harshly just because they're athletes."

Two weeks later, Alicia forwarded Autumn an incident report that described a resident being shot in the neck with a paintball gun. Andy was listed as a witness on the report but did not respond to Autumn's e-mails and phone calls regarding the situation. Other witnesses Autumn contacted said that Andy had provided the loaded paintball gun to the resident and said, "If you're going to go after big game, you need target practice."

Autumn charged Andy with a conduct code violation as an active participant in the incident and sent Andy a letter notifying him of the scheduled hearing. The next day, Autumn received an e-mail from Nate introducing himself and informing her that he would attend the hearing at Andy's request.

At the appointed time, Autumn was pleased to see that Nate accompanied Andy, who was walking slowly with crutches and had a cast on one foot. As author of the original incident report, Alicia also came for the hearing. After Autumn convened the meeting, she explained the role of an advisor to Nate. During this time, Andy shifted around in his chair and pushed his chair far away from Alicia.

Autumn asked Andy to discuss the incident and his alleged involvement

"I don't know why she," he nodded towards Alicia, "has it in for me unless it's because she's Black or I'm an athlete. I'm not going to stand for this any more. I haven't done any of the things she says I have, and I wasn't even there when the guy got hit with the paintball. When the guy who lives down the hall from me gets written up for noise or anything else, nothing ever happens to him. But when she thinks I'm involved in something, she goes for the jugular. My dad called his lawyer today, and it looks like he'll probably have to bring him up here to get

this straightened out. I'm tired of this place. Maybe I'll just leave and start over somewhere else."

What should Autumn do and why?

Random Threat

Craig Chatriand and Michelle Boettcher
Iowa State University

Jude is a second-year hall director at Lucas College, a midsize, public baccalaureate institution in Colorado. Jude oversees a coeducational residence hall of 450 students in suite-style rooms. Each suite is comprised of two double rooms joined by a shared bathroom.

One afternoon, Jude received a call from Lucas College's Coordinator for Student Conduct, Jerry, asking what Jude knew about a threat made in his building. When Jude replied that he had not heard about any such incident, Jerry provided the student's name, David, and his room number, which Jude recognized, and continued, "David's mother called the Dean of Students, and her call was transferred to me. She said that Morris, one of David's suitemates, had threatened to kill him. David's mother has asked for assistance in getting David to safety."

Jude said, "Let me check into this now and call you back."

As Jude hung up the phone, David's RA, Adam, stopped by the hall office to check his mail. Jude asked what he knew about the situation. Adam said that when he was walking to class this morning, he saw David and asked how things were going, "And you know, David laughed and said, 'I've got to tell you about something weird that happened,' but he added that it was no big deal." Adam continued, "Someone, David thought that it was Morris, had written 'DIE' on the bathroom mirror in dry erase marker, and David said he found it this morning when he went in to shower. David said he just scrubbed it off but told his roommate, 'I think that Morris is at it again.'"

Adam said that the message wasn't directed at any of the suitemates in particular, but he suspects that Morris may still be angry with David. Morris and David had had a falling out, because David recently started dating Morris's ex-girlfriend. Morris has complained to the other suitemates that David regularly violates the visitation policy, but Morris told Adam that he didn't want to make a formal complaint—that he would take care of it himself. Adam had not seen or spoken with the other suitemates today.

Jude asked about the tone of Adam's conversation with David. Adam said that David seemed more amused or resigned than afraid. David told Adam, "Morris does weird things like this all the time. He's not serious. It's like when he insists on bringing his own roll of toilet paper into the bathroom and taking it away with him when he leaves. He's just got some quirks."

After Jude finished getting information from Adam, he received an e-mail from David's mother. She wrote, in part,

"Clearly, a threat has been made on my son's life. The other student needs to be removed from the suite immediately. I have already spoken with Jerry, and he said only that he'd look into it. But this is serious. Since you are in charge of the building, I am asking you to move this Morris out today. I've also contacted the university police, so they can formally investigate this, and I've made the college president aware of the situation, too."

What should Jude do and why?

Bending the Rules

Melissa M. Korduner and Sarah L. Latiolais
Louisiana State University

Sally recently accepted a hall director position at Mountain Lake University, a large private comprehensive university in the Southeast. After about two months of working for Mountain Lake, she realizes how important image and professionalism are to the Department of Residence Life. The standards and expectations regarding staff behavior are extremely high both on and off the job.

On a Friday afternoon, Sally received a call from Felicia, a fellow hall director who has been with the department for three years. Felicia was very stressed about her job and all of the deadlines that she faced. Because Sally was new to the department, Felicia confided in her, telling Sally that as the newest staff member, Sally was the most unbiased regarding the department, its employees, and its practices.

Felicia invited Sally to a local pub, the Cedar Bar & Grill, to unwind with a few drinks after work. The pub was popular among members of the university community and was in close proximity to the campus. Sally was a bit hesitant, saying, "Don't a lot of students go to the Cedar? I'd just rather not run into some of our students."

Felicia replied, "It's okay. I've gone to the Cedar lots of times, and it's mostly a faculty and staff crowd."

Sally, thinking that a night out would do her good, agreed to go. Since arriving to Mountain Lake, Felicia had done much to make her feel as welcomed and comfortable as possible, and Sally believed she could return the favor and be there for her colleague. Felicia agreed to pick Sally up at 7 p.m.

While on their way home after a few drinks, a university police officer pulled Felicia's car over. Suspecting intoxication, the officer asked both women to step out of the car. As Felicia and Sally got out of Felicia's car, Officer Bates recognized Felicia as the hall director for Hyde Hall. He asked her if she was okay and she began to cry, fearing that she would be arrested and lose her license, not to mention her job. After talking briefly with the two women, Officer Bates determined that Felicia was stressed but was okay to drive her car safely and issued her a verbal warning. Feeling embarrassed, Felicia thanked the officer, and she and Sally continued home. Felicia asked Sally not to mention the incident to anyone in the department.

The following morning, the department staff was gathered for their regular weekly meeting. Steven, hall director for Trenton Hall, sat down next to Sally and asked, "Were you and Felicia pulled over last night by Officer Bates? George, my hall council president, mentioned that he saw the two of you outside Felicia's car.

What happened?" Looking a bit flustered, Sally was just about to answer when the director began the meeting, informing the staff that Felicia would not be attending as she was not feeling well.

What should Sally do and why?

6

Student Cocurricular and Greek Life Cases

Judicial Affairs and Star Athletes

Heather Rowan-Kenyon
University of Virginia

Yolanda is in her second year as the director of Judicial Affairs at Canfield State University (CSU), a large, comprehensive state institution in the eastern United States. CSU has a storied basketball history as a member of one of the top sports conferences in the nation and winner of three national championships in the last ten years. Coach Redd has been the head basketball coach for over 20 years and is a local hero. The basketball season starts in two weeks, and responsibility for claiming the conference title is perceived to rest on the shoulders of star point guard and 19-year old sophomore John. John has been touted in the area as a player with NBA potential who has escaped the poverty and drugs prevalent in the area where he grew up.

On Friday morning, as Yolanda was reviewing CSU police reports from the night before, she saw one that CSU police had forwarded but that had been originally filed by a Canfield city police officer. The police report stated that on Thursday night, John was in front of a local nightspot and, according to witnesses, was intoxicated and arguing loudly with another CSU student, Rob. John punched Rob in the face, and when Rob fell to the ground, John grabbed him by the head and told him never to argue with him again. A bystander had called 911 from his cell phone when the argument started, and an officer arrived in time to see John walking away as Rob lay on the ground with a gash near his left eye and the beginnings of a black eye becoming evident. John, who had no visible injuries, was taken into custody by police, charged with criminal assault, and released later that evening when Rob, who had been transported to the emergency room at the local hospital, assured officers that he did not want to press charges.

When Yolanda finished reading the report, she asked her administrative assistant to contact Rob and ask that he come to her office as soon as he could today. Then Yolanda's phone rang. The caller identified himself as Sam Jones, John's attorney, and asked, "When can we meet today to talk about this thing with John? There's no reason to make a big deal of it, and I think between the two of us, we can take care of it."

Yolanda knew enough about CSU athletics to recall that Sam had been a star CSU basketball player during the mid-1960s who now regularly appeared in newspaper photographs with Coach Redd at CSU athletics events. Yolanda replied, "What we can talk about is the process that will be involved and the role of attorneys in our procedures. Can I tell you more about that? The general information is also on our web site."

Sam said, "But it doesn't need to come to that. If we can meet today, we can take care of this."

Yolanda again offered to describe the processes, and Sam asked about meeting with her at 1p.m. Yolanda declined and ended the call.

Yolanda saw that a call had come in while she had been on the phone with Sam, so she checked her voicemail. There was a message from Coach Redd, saying, "Yolanda, this is Coach Redd. I know what's going on, and I want to talk to you about John's situation. I'm on my way over there right now, so don't go anywhere, okay? I'll be there in just a few minutes, and we can talk through this."

As she hung up the phone, Yolanda looked up to see her administrative assistant in her doorway, who said, "One of Rob's roommates told me that he had gone home for the weekend already. He gave me Rob's phone number at home in case you want to call him there." She handed Yolanda a piece of paper. "And a reporter from the student newspaper is waiting in the lobby to speak to you about John. Coach Redd just came in, too, and he wants to speak with you as well."

As her administrative assistant returned to her own desk, Yolanda heard, through her partly open door, a voice say, "Coach Redd, do you have any comments about the incident last night involving John?"

She then heard Coach Redd's voice: "So you're with the student newspaper? I think we've all got to keep an open mind on this. I think there's a good chance that it was just an unfortunate disagreement between two students, especially since the kid didn't want to press charges. What happens now will affect John's whole life, not just his basketball career. And if John doesn't play this season, he won't get the notice and the spotlight that he's worked so hard to earn. He's contributed so much to CSU, and it would be disappointing if we all didn't recognize that. He must be treated fairly. He's never been in trouble before."

What should Yolanda do and why?

Silent Auction

Tamie Klumpyan
St. Norbert College

James is the director of service learning at Clive College, a private, Lutheran, liberal arts college of 1,500 in the Midwestern U.S. Over the course of James's two years working at Clive—and under the president's direction—the campus community has engaged in self-study and realignment activities to affirm its mission and institutional values which center on moral convictions, personal integrity, social justice, and dignity of all persons. The service learning office has become a centerpiece of putting these values into action through its sponsorship of Student Service Trips during winter and spring breaks that focus on social justice, health, and environmental projects such as combating homelessness and domestic violence, inner city education, trail and river clean up, and HIV/AIDS education and prevention. The students involved in the trips participate in pretrip training and education on the topic of their respective trips and return to campus with strategies for educating their peers about what they learned. The trips have become extremely popular, with more than 200 students participating in last year's ten trips.

To subsidize the cost of the service trip program, a six-person student committee with James as the advisor plans and coordinates an annual fundraising dinner and silent auction. The planning committee for this event identified committee members to serve as coordinators for the following areas: recruitment and supervision of volunteer chefs, recruitment of student groups for setup, decorations and cleanup, emcee and entertainment selection, and soliciting donations for the silent auction. This year's committee also plans to include some of the past trip participants' stories and pictures in the dinner and auction program.

James has concluded that in his two years at Clive, this year's committee is one of the best. The students are not only organized and dedicated to the planning, but most are past participants of the trips and are committed to creating social change and promoting justice. They appear to really believe in the program and are enthusiastically working to ensure its continued financial viability.

At the third committee meeting, Leila, the student coordinator responsible for soliciting prizes for the silent auction, shared a list of her most recent donations. Among her list is a $50.00 gift certificate from JUGS, which describes itself as "a restaurant and bar for those looking to socialize." JUGS is famous for its $3.00 jugs of beer, hot wings, and attractive female service staff. During recent years, some community members and Clive students had vocally shared their concerns about what they believed to be the establishment's exploitation of women. Leila briefly noted and discussed each donation and then wrapped up her report with an announcement that a respected and popular artist in the community had donated a drawing that would be reasonably valued at several hundred dollars.

The student committee appeared excited about the numerous donations and, in particular, the artwork and praised Leila for her hard work and persistence. Jon, the committee chair noted that, under Leila's leadership, the number and value of donations had far exceeded their expectations. No further mention was made of the JUGS certificate during the meeting.

After the meeting, James asked Leila to speak with him for a minute. "Leila, I have some real concerns about the JUGS gift certificate. How do you square this prize with the mission and values of the college that we're always discussing here on campus?"

Leila replied, "I guess I don't see it as that big a problem. I think we need to provide a wide variety of auction items for the diverse audience that we want to attend this event. And this gift certificate will draw a large bid that will go directly to underwriting the service trips. Besides, James, the women who work there make the choice to work there. And the jobs are reasonably well paying, too, for part-time work, not like the minimum-wage jobs that are mostly available around here for students and other young people."

During his regular meeting with Nancy, the associate dean of students, James apprised her of progress on the fundraiser and mentioned the JUGS donation and his conversation with Leila. Nancy replied, "What do you recommend we do?"

What should James do and why?

Anonymous Allegations

Heather Rowan-Kenyon
University of Virginia

Lance is in his first year as the fraternity advisor at Eastern State University, a large research institution on the east coast. This is Lance's first professional job, although he completed two half-time internship experiences in Greek affairs as part of his master's degree program. Approximately 20% of ESU's students are members of a national fraternity or a sorority. Late one Friday afternoon, Lance received a call from a parent who wanted to remain anonymous but was very concerned about his son, who was going through the new member process in a fraternity on campus.

The parent stated, "I'm really unhappy with my son's pledging experience. He's been forced to drink and do calisthenics for long periods of time over the last few weeks. And they expect him to be a gofer for his big brother. He's been forced to clean his big brother's room in the chapter house and do his laundry. The latest thing, which is ridiculous, is that he hasn't been allowed to sleep or shower over the last two days, since the beginning of hell week. The whole thing is just absurd! And my son's really concerned now about his homework with papers and tests coming down the road."

The parent then shared that members of the chapter had laughed and told his son that things were just going to get worse as the week goes on, and that there was a big event scheduled for that evening. The father continued, "Now, I don't want my son to know that I've called you. He wants to stick it out, since he came this far."

At Lance's request, the father revealed the name of the chapter, Alpha Alpha Alpha, but again refused to give his son's name. Lance glanced down at his office phone and noticed the Caller ID window displaying a phone number, which he quickly jotted down on a note pad. The area code was one that covered the northeastern part of the state. Lance then asked the father to describe some of the activities in more detail, but the father replied, "That's all I know. Isn't that enough?"

Lance again asked for the student's name, telling the father that in order to be able to investigate the situation quickly, and because the chapter's big event was scheduled for that evening, it would be helpful to contact the student directly. The father said, "Look, I promised my son that I'd let him get through this, but this whole thing seems ridiculous to me. I just want you to take a look at what's going on up there, and you don't need my son's name for that! Why do you allow this kind of thing at ESU?"

Alpha Alpha Alpha is the oldest fraternity on campus. Three buildings on campus are named after alumni who belonged to this chapter, and ESU's president, Dr. Smith, is a brother. In the short time that Lance has been on campus, he has built a good relationship with the chapter's president, Tim, who is committed to ending new member hazing. In one recent conversation, Tim told Lance reluctantly that some of his fellow chapter officers don't seem to be as invested in this goal.

Lance took all the information from the phone call to his supervisor, Bob, the director of Greek Life. It was already close to 5 p.m., so Lance was relieved to see that Bob had not yet left for the weekend. Bob had been director for ten years and was good friends with Alpha Alpha Alpha's advisor, Matt O'Donnell. Bob said he was slightly concerned about the report but wondered if it is true, since the caller would not identify himself or his son. Bob told Lance that, nonetheless, he would take care of it. He was playing golf with Matt in the morning and would mention it to him then. Bob added, "I know that Matt will deal effectively with this, so you don't need to worry about it."

Lance asked Bob if tomorrow would be too late, since the father had said that the "big event" was planned for that evening. Bob responded, "Well, I really don't think so. Chapter members say things like that just to try to scare the new guys. Don't worry about it. Enjoy your weekend."

Even with Bob's reassurance, Lance decided to call Tim to ask what the chapter had going on this weekend, but Tim's cell phone rolled to voicemail after his recorded greeting of "Hi, I'm on a well-deserved weekend away from it all, but I'll call you back Monday." Lance stopped by Bob's office again on his way home, but Bob had already left.

What should Lance do and why?

Painted Signs

Karla Carney
Cornell College

Sarianna is the student activities coordinator at Heritage College, a small, private, residential, liberal arts college. One of the fixtures in the center of campus is a three-pillared kiosk that individual students and student organizations regularly paint with announcements about events, political issues, and other signs of support, dissent, or commentary. The kiosk is located on a main pedestrian walkway between a residence hall and the student union in a high traffic area. The Student Code of Conduct describes the kiosk as one of three spaces on campus that can be painted at will, implying a free speech space. Although there are no stated rules governing the kiosk, a general agreement among students has emerged that, as a courtesy to others, one should wait 24 hours before painting over a side of the kiosk. In the case of an advertised event, one should wait until after the event has taken place. Generally, administrative office representatives do not paint the kiosk unless it is in conjunction with a major campus event like orientation or homecoming.

Sarianna had concluded that the system seemed to work well, and the kiosk continued to be well utilized by students. In her two years at Heritage, no real problems had surfaced other than students' ongoing concerns about the haste with which they have to claim a side of the kiosk to paint. One group that made frequent use of the kiosk was the Gay Lesbian Bisexual Transgender Alliance (GLBTA), a student group particularly interested in the politics of gender on campus. The GLBTA faculty advisor was not actively involved with the group in accordance with his belief that it should have ultimate autonomy as a political organization. However, the campus diversity office worked closely with all student organizations to emphasize topics and projects related to diversity and inclusion.

Recently, one of the GLBTA members found a media campaign on the Internet called "Fuk Your Gender" that challenged sex and gender stereotypes. The group decided to initiate a related week-long media campaign on campus that would start with painting the kiosk. To advertise the campaign's Monday kick-off event, early on Friday afternoon, GLBTA members painted one side of the kiosk with "Fuk Your Gender" and "Starts Monday, 3 p.m., Commons. Be there."

On that same Friday around 4:00 p.m., Sarianna received a phone call from George, the director of admissions, who said, "Listen, I just heard about the kiosk, and we need to do something about it now, Sarianna. I know that this group is entitled to use the space same as other groups, but don't you remember that we're starting one of our Heritage Weekends this afternoon? Our office has almost 200 prospective students and family members coming for campus tours, recruitment programs, and entertainment. I would ask some of my student volunteers or staff to come and paint it over, but they're all out meeting families at the airport or doing final preparations for the opening reception later today. Can't you help me out here? Would you find a couple of students who can paint the kiosk now before any more families arrive on campus?"

When Sarianna informed George of the general agreements and practices surrounding the kiosk, George replied, "You have to realize that these weekends are tremendous opportunities to showcase Heritage and make a favorable impression. What's on the kiosk now is a major distraction—if not also terribly offensive to the guests who we've invited to visit us. So again, I'm asking you to get this painted over. We can deal with any fallout on Monday."

What should Sarianna do and why?

Must the Show Go On?

W. Houston Dougharty
Lewis and Clark College

Kim is so excited that her student concert programmers have been able to book one of the coolest indie bands around, Sir Knee's Solid Hairy Hose. Ever since Kim took the programming staff to the regional National Association for Campus Activities (NACA) conference—where they first heard the band live—it's been the goal of the staff to sign this group as the closing act for the annual spring festival on campus. Even though the band's agent was evasive and tough to work with, Kim and her programmers are eager to see the concert happen.

Kim arrived three years ago at Graydon College, a small, West Coast, liberal arts college campus just out of her student affairs master's program. When she arrived, one of her main goals as director of activities was to gain the trust of student government leaders and the programmers they hire every year. Student government and its programming have always played a strong role on this suburban campus of 2,000 undergraduate and 300 graduate students.

This year's student staff is the best Kim has ever seen—in part because she has been able to supervise a couple of them as student employees and mentor the others as they've volunteered and worked their way up into lead programming positions. The year has been a terrific success: booking a famous comedian who's currently starring in her own T.V. sitcom; hosting the regional College Bowl competition; collaborating with the theatre department to host a traveling Broadway musical; and offering lots of smaller concerts with regional and local blues, rock, alternative, and jazz bands. But, the Sir Knee's Solid Hairy Hose concert will be the biggest event of the year, with cosponsorship by the most popular local FM station.

The day of the concert arrived. All the programmers and volunteers arrived on time at the gymnasium for load in, and the setup for the show went perfectly. Kim learned from the student ticket manager that the show was sold out and that the radio station was being barraged with calls and e-mails for ticket giveaways. This was really coming together beautifully!

The band arrived, along with their manager, who seemed impatient and tersely barked some orders to the students doing the final setup. The band got settled into the green room (a locker room that the programmers outfitted with couches, a deli spread, and a stereo). As the campus warm-up band began to play its 30-minute set to the packed gym, the band's manager found Kim in the hallway and asked, "So where's the booze?"

Kim was shocked at his question and replied, "Alcohol isn't allowed at campus events. That's policy."

He angrily retorted, "Oh, come on!! I was clear with your programmers that this requirement wasn't negotiable. The band won't play without drinks in the green room and on stage. This is your last chance: drinks now, or we pack up and leave."

Kim noticed that two of her programmers had overheard this exchange. One of them, trying to help resolve the situation, came over to Kim and the band's manager and said, "I've got some stuff in my room that I can bring over. It'll just take a minute."

What should Kim do and why?

Student Activities Program Assessment

Sean Grube
Rockhurst University

The Southern University (TSU) is a comprehensive, four-year, public institution in the Southeast with an enrollment of approximately 30,000 undergraduate and graduate students. TSU is a regular contender for its conference's football championship, and a culture of alcohol consumption has surrounded each home game. The worst nights for excessive student drinking are usually the Fridays before home football games when an influx of friends, visitors, and alumni come to the city to indulge before the next day's game. Four years ago, to combat the excessive partying that accompanies the games, the Department of Student Activities (DSA) debuted Southern Nights. Southern Nights is held five times each fall on the nights prior to each home football game and provides a substance-free alternative for TSU students. Southern Nights are consistently the most well attended programs that the DSA sponsors throughout the year, and the TSU Parents' Association has donated $25,000 per year for each of the past three years, with the possibility of extending the funding pending a formal assessment of the impact of the program over its first three years.

Kianna joined the DSA immediately after graduating with her master's degree six months ago, and she is a student activities coordinator. She had been asked to join the Southern Nights assessment committee consisting of a substance abuse coordinator from the TSU health center, a graduate intern in the DSA, a judicial affairs coordinator in the Dean of Students office, and the committee chair, Roberta, who is also the DSA director and Kianna's immediate supervisor. The assessment committee was charged with creating a report that Roberta will present to the Parent's Association to seek not only their continued funding but also additional support to broaden the scope of the program. Kianna understood that this report will be based on the committee's analysis of surveys and additional data from students who had attended two or more Southern Nights programs during the past year.

A subcommittee's initial data analyses revealed that, while the program is immensely popular and extremely well attended, students' excessive drinking before home games has continued. A large proportion of students who were surveyed explained that they attend Southern Nights events for free food and the chance to socialize with others before heading downtown to the bars and clubs afterward to party. Supplemental data confirmed these findings, with the numbers of alcohol-related incidents on these nights holding steady or increasing slightly since the inception of Southern Nights.

At the next committee meeting, the subcommittee presented these findings to the entire committee and then listened to objections by committee members. Leroy, the judicial affairs coordinator, offered, "The program is fulfilling its purpose by providing a substance-free alternative to students. That's what it is supposed to do, and that's what it does, period."

Josh, the graduate intern, commented, "My understanding of our task is that we needed to find out if the program is successful and run efficiently. That's what we asked about, and we found out that it is."

The subsequent discussion got extremely heated, and Roberta ended the meeting with no real decision on the issue.

Roberta e-mailed Kianna and the rest of the committee about a quick committee meeting that she's arranged for the next day. Roberta wrote, "I need to identify and rehearse my talking points for the Parents' Association. As you know, I'll be presenting our findings at their meeting this Thursday." When all were present for the meeting, Roberta began, "You know that Southern Nights is a really important program for TSU. While there appear to be shortcomings, I'm confident that improvements can be made in the near future. Now, how can I best convey this at the Parents' Association meeting?"

What should Kianna do and why?

Student Activity Petty Cash

Matthew R. Shupp
Community College of Philadelphia

Roger recently graduated with his master's degree in higher education and accepted his first professional position at Coldsprings College, a midsize, public, baccalaureate state institution that enrolls approximately 10,000 students. The Office of Student Activities, a department in the Division of Student Affairs, recently underwent organizational changes, and Roger is arriving to the campus to fill a newly created position. Previously, the office was staffed by a director and assistant director of Student Activities, along with one administrative assistant. As the new Coordinator of clubs and organizations, Roger works out of the Student Union Building (SUB) and reports directly to the assistant director of Student Activities. His primary responsibilities include advising the 30 largest student clubs and organizations and ensuring proper usage of the student fee funds allocated to each club. One of his largest groups, the Student Programming Board (SPB), is in charge of the immensely popular and well-attended weekly campus film series.

Roger's direct supervisor, Maureen, has been at the institution for several years and, prior to the staffing changes, had advised the clubs that Roger now advises. His relationship with Maureen thus far has been positive. He feels comfortable discussing new and innovative ideas with her and has gotten used to her candid style and her enjoyment of animated brainstorming sessions.

Members of the SPB have recently approached Roger with a new idea concerning the $1.00 admission fee charged to students attending the Friday night films. In the past, the money collected at the door was counted by the SPB representative, matched to the ticket sales, and then turned over to Roger for deposit into the SPB account. The Student Activities budget pays for the film licenses, and the revenue collected from ticket sales is used to purchase snacks and drinks for students during the film. Previously, members of the SPB would go shopping for these snacks and drinks, pay for the food with their own money, and then submit receipts to Roger for reimbursement. Since many of the students were paying their own tuition or had loans, there was often a lengthy discussion as to who would have to go grocery shopping. The SPB students proposed setting up a petty cash fund, so they would no longer have to spend their own money and wait to get reimbursed. They proposed that $100.00 in cash be held in the Student Activities area to cover such costs.

Roger liked the idea and discussed it with Maureen. She agreed and proposed that the petty cash be kept locked in a filing cabinet in her office. Appropriate arrangements were made, and the SPB members were informed about the steps needed to access petty cash funds.

The new petty cash system had been working well for a few months until one afternoon Roger knocked on Maureen's door to request access to the petty cash. The SPB members had filed a formal request for $100.00 to purchase snacks this evening. A very popular movie was being shown this weekend, and advance ticket sales had been brisk. Maureen told Roger, "Oh my gosh, Roger, I completely forgot about this! I had to borrow $80.00 the other night for sort of a personal emergency. I'll get the $80.00 back in the petty cash box tomorrow."

What should Roger do and why?

Disclosure of Hazing

Matthew D. Pistilli
Purdue University

Deborah J. Taub
University of North Carolina-Greensboro

Brian, in his first job out of graduate school, accepted a position as a hall director at Great Plains State University (GPSU). GPSU is a rural, midsize, comprehensive public university with an enrollment of about 10,000. Roughly 3,500 students live on campus in one of GPSU's 16 residence halls, and 1,500 of these students are affiliated with a Greek letter organization that has a designated residence hall floor or wing. The Department of Residence Life employs full-time hall directors with master's degrees to supervise the residence halls. Each hall director supervises two halls and 12 to 15 RAs. Brian is working with an RA staff that was hired by his predecessor; he had never been a hall director prior to accepting this position.

Brian's first year on the job as a hall director at GPSU was rather tumultuous, with some staff changes, some animosity among his RAs, and a heavy judicial caseload. It also was his first time supervising a staff, and he found it to be something of a challenge. Now it is March, and things are running more smoothly. Brian was waiting in the lobby of one of his halls to meet with Heather, one of his RAs, for their biweekly one-on-one supervision meeting. Heather is a sophomore, an exemplary first-year RA, and an officer in her sorority.

Heather arrived in the lobby in conversation with a group of friends. She was talking—rather loudly—about her sorority, which was starting to wrap up their spring new member activities. Heather was describing in some detail one recent evening when pledges had all put condoms on bananas and lip synched songs using the bananas as microphones. She also talked about the night she and her sorority's members had told blindfolded pledges that they were about to be fed a live fish, and how they asked pledges to recite the Greek alphabet while the rest of the members turned out the lights and shot water guns and silly string at them. Heather and her friends laughed as they said goodbye.

As Brian and Heather headed toward their meeting, he inquired, "I heard you talking just now, and what you described sounds like hazing to me."

Heather acknowledged that some of the things they'd done "probably sound like hazing when you just say them out loud like that" and that some "could maybe be perceived as hazing" as well. "But," she replied earnestly, "I don't know how it could be hazing. No one is getting hurt, and we're just having fun. Besides, the sorority has been doing these exact same activities with pledges for as long as any of the seniors can remember. Our alumni advisors know about them too, and they would never condone hazing. And the girls all know that they can stop participating whenever they want—we tell them that every time we start pledging activities."

Brian asked, "What happens to the women who stop participating?"

Heather replied quickly, "None of the girls have ever said, 'No.' And anyway, it's all just fun. We would hate to have sisters who aren't willing to have a little bit of fun."

What should Brian do and why?

Lee and the CEE Party

Joshua Hiscock
Roger Williams University

Lee, 22, is a recent college graduate who relocated to another state soon after completing her undergraduate degree to enter the master's program in college student personnel at Southwest University, a public, research institution of approximately 26,000 students. She is now a graduate assistant in the Office of Student Activities, and as part of her responsibilities there serves as coadvisor to Campus Entertainment Events (CEE), the student-run programming group at Southwest. Sam, a second-year graduate assistant (GA) in the office, is CEE's coadvisor, and Amie, who is full-time in the office, supervises Lee and Sam. Over 100 students apply for the 25 CEE programmer slots each year, and those selected are among the most highly involved student leaders. Lee directly advises the five student programmers who coordinate campus lectures and visiting speakers. She meets with this group on a weekly basis to plan activities, brainstorm new programming ideas, and coordinate logistics for events. The remaining 20 students are advised by Sam or Amie. Lee also informally interacts one-on-one with most of the 25 students on weekdays, as CEE programmers hold their mandatory office hours down the hall from Lee's office.

During the fall semester, which was also Lee's first semester in the master's program, she had established a comfortable rapport with the students, often talking with them about their personal lives and their experiences outside of CEE. At rare times, she had discussed her recent undergraduate experiences, some of the loneliness associated with moving to a new university, and her recent breakup with a significant other that had resulted from her move. While Lee's informal conversations with the students were usually social in nature, some of the students had spoken with her about personal issues like relationship issues or life decision challenges, including one student who was seriously considering dropping out of school because she was confused about her major: she'd changed it three times in the last semester and had not found a good fit through any of those changes. Lee always assured her students that their conversations would be held in confidence.

One Thursday afternoon, one of Lee's students, Sally, gave Lee a folded invitation to a party that some of the CEE students planned off campus for Friday night. The invitation, complete with an amended CEE logo that read "Celebration of Endangered Ecstasies" billed the party as, "the hottest, highest, most exciting CEE event of the semester!"

Sally told Lee that, because of her comfortable rapport and approachable nature, she thought Lee would be cool with the idea and wanted to invite her to hang out with everyone in a more social setting, because she felt that Lee would enjoy getting loose with everyone and making some new friends. Somewhat flustered, Lee thanked Sally for the invitation and watched as Sally left the office. Doing a quick calculation in her head, based on the class standing of the CEE directors, Lee estimated that nine of the 25 programmers in the organization were 21 or older, and Sally was not one of them. And drug use was illegal regardless of age.

What should Lee do and why?

Hazing Hits Home

Lori Patton
Iowa State University

Angela has recently completed her master's degree in student affairs at Alpha University and has accepted a full-time position at her undergraduate alma mater, Dowling State University (DSU). DSU is a predominantly White, midsize, public, comprehensive institution located in the Midwest. The total student enrollment at DSU is 19,000. The students at DSU are highly involved in over 300 student organizations. The Greek letter community has the largest number of student participants, since almost 15% of all undergraduate students are affiliated with a sorority or fraternity. The Greek community at DSU is comprised of the individual chapters and four councils: Panhellenic Council, Interfraternity Council, National Pan-Hellenic Council, and the Multicultural Greek Council. Each council receives assistance and guidance from the Greek Affairs Office, which is staffed by one director, three assistant directors, and an office coordinator.

While in graduate school, Angela gained practical experience in advising through her assistantship in Greek Affairs. At Dowling, Angela serves as the assistant director for Greek Life Programs. She also advises the National Pan-Hellenic Council (NPHC) for historically Black sororities and fraternities and the Multicultural Greek Council, which represents the Latino/a and Asian American Greek letter organizations. Angela is extremely excited about working at Dowling because of her familiarity with the campus and her previous experience as a Greek student leader. As a member of Gamma Omega Epsilon (ΓOE), one of four Black sororities at Dowling, she was chapter president during her senior year. Under her leadership, the chapter received the Student Organization of the Year award and the Highest Grade Point Average award.

When the fall semester began, Angela felt more than ready to begin her new position. During the second week of classes, Carolyn, the current president of ΓOE and one of the women who Angela had initiated, came by Angela's office. After they exchanged greetings, Carolyn said, "All of us in ΓOE are really excited to have you back at Dowling, so we can continue to benefit from your great leadership. You know that we've continued your high standards for ΓOE by being an outstanding chapter with a stellar reputation on campus. We want to select new members who are committed to excellence. So far this year, we've met with nine women who are interested in ΓOE. We'd really like for you to meet with them, too, and give us your advice on who you think would be good members. When would be a good time for us to schedule this meeting?"

Angela smiled briefly, thanked Carolyn for stopping by, and told her she'd get back to her. Carolyn then left for class. Angela closed her office door and sat down in her chair with a sigh. Ever since she had decided to take the position at

Dowling, she had wondered if this might happen. Angela vividly recalled her own participation in hazing activities as an undergraduate, believing at the time that hazing was the way to gain respect among peers and to continue traditions. At the time, she had not seriously thought about the ramifications of hazing even though she knew it was against university policy; she considered it tradition, since no one ever complained or seemed concerned about it.

However, her experiences in graduate school in particular had helped her learn much more about hazing, its dangerous consequences, and the illegality of the activity. Angela was now firmly opposed to hazing. However, during Angela's student days at Dowling, "meeting with prospective members" had often been the phrase used to invite someone's participation in hazing—or at least to witness activities that, at the time, would have constituted hazing. Angela realized that her chapter was welcoming her continued involvement in their traditional activities despite her professional role on campus.

What should Angela do and why?

A Gift for Leadership

Hilton Hallock and Christopher Foley
University of Pennsylvania

Flordon College (FC) is a small, historically Black college that prides itself on a high level of student engagement in cocurricular activities. One of the most active undergraduate students at FC, Elizabeth, was president of her sorority, an admissions tour guide, and the founder of a major service initiative at the college. After graduating from FC, she earned a master's degree in higher education administration and worked for three years as a program coordinator in the Office of Student Activities at a large state university. Elizabeth has recently returned to FC as the director of the Leadership Center.

The Leadership Center is part of the student life office and was founded two years ago with startup money from the college's Parents' Program. Elizabeth's staff position was incorporated into the Student Life budget, but money is short at FC and no additional money was earmarked for leadership programming. Like most other Student Life programs, all activities must be cosponsored or self-supporting.

Soon after her arrival, Elizabeth met with her supervisor, Pat, the dean of Student Life, to identify priorities for the Leadership Center. The most pressing need discussed was funding for leadership development programs. Pat said, "I'm concerned that the Center isn't providing enough outreach. As director, you also must secure funding streams for workshops, speakers, library resources, and marketing the center's services. These are going to be seen as the indicators of your success as the director of this center."

Another pressing concern Pat identified was a problem she called the "redundancy of leadership" in student organizations. The same students occupied multiple leadership positions, thus limiting opportunities for others to be involved in leadership. Pat noted that the Greek system, which at FC is comprised of chapters representing four National Pan-Hellenic Council (NPHC) organizations, had a monopoly on student leadership positions. The chapters took seriously their missions as leadership and service organizations, and affiliated students had been more active and organized in student-run election processes. Nonetheless, it was clear to Elizabeth that she must engage a broader pool of students in leadership development activities and successfully raise money for her initiatives.

After determining her priorities, Elizabeth met with Henry, a representative of FC's Development Office, to discuss the possibility of raising funds to meet the needs of the center. They brainstormed a number of possible gifts, including an endowment for a speaker series and corporate sponsorship for an emerging leaders' conference. Although Henry made no promises, he was optimistic that some prospective donors might be drawn to the opportunity to help students develop their leadership potential. He also warned her, "Cultivating donors can take a long time, so be prepared."

Henry arranged for Elizabeth to address two alumni groups in her first semester as Director. Much to her surprise, after the second event, Elizabeth received a message from Henry saying that he had identified a prospective donor. An FC alumna who heard Elizabeth's address was very excited about the Leadership Center. The prospective donor had been a student leader herself, and she wanted to endow FC's Student Leader Development Fund to assist the center. However, as a condition of the gift, the donor has stipulated that the fund must be used to sponsor leadership activities for active members of NPHC organizations.

What should Elizabeth do and why?

Student Activity Funding

Molly Pavlechko
Bucknell University

Ellington College is a small, highly selective, four-year, liberal arts institution. The quaint campus is nestled in a rural New England town. As a coeducational residential college, Ellington allows students a unique opportunity to create a rich social life to complement their rigorous academic courses. Kirsten recently received her master's degree in college student personnel and began her job as assistant director of student programming at Ellington soon after graduation. Her responsibilities include advising several groups, including the Student Government Association (SGA), monitoring the student clubs and organizations and assisting newly formed clubs to become officially recognized groups at EC, and offering a variety of campus activities and programs for the 1,500 undergraduate students. When she interviewed at Ellington, Kirsten had been pleased to learn that the overall racial and ethnic diversity of the student body had been steadily increasing over the last few years, and 11% of enrolled students identify themselves as members of historically underrepresented groups. When she had visited campus, all of the individuals with whom she met seemed to be sincerely committed to meeting the needs of all Ellington students, particularly students who were not used to living in rural areas or in New England.

During Kirsten's first week on the job, her supervisor, Corey, met with her for lunch and explained that, although Ellington had increased the student activity fee for the current academic year, poor returns on Ellington's endowment investments had substantially reduced the supplemental operating budgets that many offices had come to depend on over the last several years. As a result, Corey continued, "We and every other office on campus will have to keep our program costs to a minimum and postpone implementation of any new services to offset the shortfalls. We're going to have to be creative but frugal, and as part of that, you'll need to make sure to send requests through all the proper channels before making any promises to students about available resources."

Toward the end of the first semester, John and Susan, the SGA's president and treasurer, came to visit with Kirsten. Since the numbers of student clubs and organizations had been relatively stable in recent years, the SGA had always been able to approve the organizations' requests for funding. This semester, however, there was a surge of new clubs being chartered, and the student government was faced with an overwhelming demand to allocate resources for these new organizations' activities. In addition to new clubs, it seemed that current clubs were dividing into smaller groups that targeted the needs of Ellington's growing racial, ethnic, and culturally diverse student population. For example, in September the Dance Club had split into four organizations, each of which had subsequently become a recognized organization in accordance with Student Programming Office procedures: Jelani, the Latino Dance Group, the Flamenco Dancers, and the Dance Club. However, each organization then requested from SGA roughly the same budget as had previously been allocated to the original Dance Club. Susan concluded, "I just don't know how to handle this. We've run low on funds already."

The money allocated to SGA for funding clubs was taken from the student activity fee at the beginning of each academic year; therefore, SGA would not receive another allocation until the following fall. At a subsequent SGA officers' meeting, Susan again expressed her concern that too much money had been allocated so far this semester to student groups, with much of the allocations going to the newer and smaller organizations. She recommended that the SGA reserve a large portion of the remaining money for the spring semester because, she said, "We know that the Dance Club and other longstanding groups usually have made their funding requests in spring. We have to be able to meet their needs." She then turned to a draft of her treasurer's report and said, "At our current pace, we'll be out of money by February."

John shook his head and turned to Kirsten, "Isn't there such a thing as too many clubs, especially at a college this size and since the funding is so limited? Can your office declare a moratorium on approving new organizations until things stabilize?"

Kirsten explained that all groups meeting requirements to be recognized organizations must be recognized, that she could not draw distinctions. She added, "But SGA should certainly determine a set of priorities and guidelines that will help you make fair and defensible allocations to student groups."

At the next SGA meeting, the student government received a request for funding from the newly recognized African American Women's Accounting Club, and the request was denied.

Joanna, the club's president, came to visit Kirsten the following day, and said, "I can't believe that we're not worthy of even some support. That money comes from our fees, too. I asked John after the meeting what some other options might be for us, and he said we should be a subgroup of the Accounting Club. Doesn't he realize that the Accounting Club was where this group started, but we weren't being taken seriously? Oh, and John also suggested that maybe we could charge membership dues for the first couple of years to see whether the group would really be viable. I don't know of any other group on campus that does this. Why should we? This isn't right, and I have a letter to the editor ready to send to the campus newspaper. We shouldn't have to put up with this kind of treatment."

What should Kirsten do and why?

Greek Week Awards

Jennifer Plagman-Galvin
Iowa State University

Annie is in her second year as Greek advisor at Alpha State University, a large public institution where the Greek community consists of 20 chapters, most of which have houses on or near Greek Row. In addition to her work with chapters, officers, and members, Annie maintained regular contact with chapters' alumni advisors. She also advised the Interfraternity Council (IFC), National Pan-Hellenic Council (NPHC), Panhellenic Council (PC), Order of Omega, and the Executive Council that planned the ASU's annual Greek Week event.

Greek Week is held every March to highlight the Greek community's contributions and to emphasize the four pillars of the Greek community: philanthropy, scholarship, leadership, and friendship. At ASU, Greek Week has included intramural sports, academic recognitions, talent contests, service projects, social events, and the Greek Olympics—a combination of serious and humorous games and relays. Greek Week awards are given to chapters or teams of chapters who win the individual events. Winners of additional awards, such as the Founder's Award for the chapter that best exemplified the ideals of Greek Week and the four pillars, are determined by the Executive Council. The Sunday Awards Banquet is the final event of each Greek Week.

Last spring's Greek Week had been quite successful, but Annie had been concerned by the relatively low participation by individual chapter members. She saw that subsets of more active members had been stretched thin preparing for and participating in Greek Week. Annie had subsequently set a goal to encourage all individual members' participation in one or more aspects of Greek Week and to try to build a spirit of community and common purpose that would involve all of the chapters. She had discussed these perspectives with the Greek Week cochairs, Sarah and Matt, as soon as they had been selected last April, and both students had voiced enthusiasm for this goal.

Sarah and Matt had accomplished most of the organizational preplanning during the summer months, and in September, Annie advised them on broad and systematic recruitment strategies to identify candidates for the Executive Council from the individual chapters. Matt stopped by Annie's office one afternoon and said, "You really were right about recruitment. We have 22 applicants for the 10 Exec Council slots. See you this evening."

Annie asked Matt to clarify "this evening," and he replied, "Oh, Sarah said last week she would ask you to come to the Exec Council interviews. Half are tonight and half are tomorrow night. Can you be there?"

Annie agreed, and Matt said he would bring copies of all the applications for Annie tonight, since he didn't have them with him. Later that day, Sarah called

Annie and said, "Matt just called me. I'm sorry that I dropped the ball on this. I'm so glad that you can make it for the interviews."

During the course of the interviews, Annie realized that the 22 applicants represented seven of the 20 chapters at ASU. After Matt and Sarah made their decisions, individuals from six chapters (two fraternities and four sororities) were appointed to the Greek Week Executive Council. No individuals from National Pan-Hellenic Council chapters had applied for Exec Council. Planning progressed throughout the fall semester. In December, the Exec Council passed a resolution that individuals from all participating chapters would pledge to be alcohol-free during Greek Week. All three governing councils (IFC, PC, and NPHC) subsequently endorsed the pledge.

Erin, an Exec Council member, suggested at a January meeting, "We've always asked a notable ASU individual to attend the banquet and present our awards. I think we should ask Dr. Henson, the Student Affairs VP. He has focused consistently on problem drinking and substance abuse among ASU students, and that would help us highlight and reinforce our alcohol free pledge."

Erin's suggestion was approved by Exec Council, and Erin later reported, "He agreed. He said he was honored to be asked, and he congratulated us on the pledge."

Annie received an e-mail from Dr. Henson expressing pleasure both with the invitation and with the commitment the chapters had made. His e-mail ended, "It's clear that you're doing a great job as Greek advisor. Thank you for your contributions and your hard work."

Annie braced herself for the flurry of activities once Greek Week began. By Saturday, she was pleased with the week's events but worried about her e-mail backlog and the growing stacks of papers and unopened mail on her desk. After attending a Greek Week event early Saturday evening, Annie spent the rest of the evening in her office, leaving for home around midnight. As she drove toward home, she noticed two young men on the sidewalk, walking erratically, laughing, and gesturing to each other wildly. She thought, "Coming home from the bars . . ." but then looked more closely as she drove past them. She recognized both as fifth year seniors and members of Matt's fraternity. As her car passed, the two men waved and called out happily, "Hey, it's Annie!"

Sunday at noon, the Executive Council met with Annie to finalize the list of Greek Week awards to be presented at the Banquet. Susanna said, "I nominate Matt's fraternity, Tau Gamma Iota, for the Founder's Award." Erin seconded Susanna's motion. Sarah nodded and said, "Any discussion?"

What should Annie do and why?

Student Entertainment

Donechanh Inthalangsy Southammavong
Des Moines Area Community College

Lynda recently graduated from her master's degree program from a university in the northeastern United States and accepted a newly created position at Northwest State University (NSU), a large public land-grant research university. In her role as an activities coordinator with MSU's Scholars Academy (SA) program, Lynda works with first-year students who are first-generation college attendees or from low socioeconomic backgrounds. The goal of SA is to provide academic and social support to smooth the students' adjustment to college and help them initiate connections with each other, with faculty members, and with staff members in various MSU resource offices. Some of Lynda's responsibilities include hosting three student/faculty socials per semester, planning a spring luncheon, meeting regularly with her assigned SA mentees, and coteaching a one-credit fall SA Orientation course. The luncheon is a celebratory banquet, and the socials combine brief information on an educational topic (such as career exploration) and some entertainment, with an opportunity for all SA students to visit informally with each other and with invited faculty members afterward. Suzanna, Lynda's graduate assistant, planned and coteaches the other section of the SA Orientation course. SA students are required to attend all of these events, so now that it is midway through fall semester, Lynda feels like she is getting to know most of the SA students quite well.

One of these students, Jay, has become a very enthusiastic participant in the SA program after a somewhat lackluster academic start at MSU. His midterm grade reports confirmed the shaky start, but Lynda has seen some of his more recent assignments and feels that his academic work is now stronger. He spends a good bit of his free time during the week at the SA office visiting with SA staff and other students, and he often studies there, using a desk in a vacant office. He is pleasant and friendly, and staff members enjoy his visits. Based on his initial difficult transition of moving from a large city several hours away, the many friends he has made in the last two months, and his academic improvement, Lynda views Jay as one of the SA program's success stories in the making.

Jay is also one of Lynda's mentees, and during their last meeting, he proudly told Lynda that he and three other MSU students from his residence hall have formed a singing group. He said that they have started to perform for small gatherings on campus and asked if his group could perform for one of the SA socials. Lynda had begun to plan the third social of the semester, which would focus on sustaining one's academic focus, and she invited Jay to perform one song between the formal program and the informal social portion of the event. He immediately accepted and assured Lynda that the group would practice very hard. The morning of the social, Jay e-mailed Lynda to tell her that he was really looking forward to having his group perform. Lynda smiled at the e-mail, thinking that this would be a wonderful opportunity for Jay to demonstrate his talent and perhaps motivate and inspire his peers.

After MSU's academic support coordinator finished his remarks to the assembled group of SA students and invited faculty members, Lynda introduced Jay. Wild applause and calls followed from the students. Lynda stood off to one side, and listened as Jay and the three other students started their recorded music and rapped:

If you wanna live for the world, just live it up.

Smoke it up, drink it up, live it up, sex it up.

But if you wanna live for Christ, just give it up.

Give it up, pray up, so you can stay up!

At the end of their song, Jay stepped forward and announced a student-run Bible study that was being held the following evening in his residence hall, "Everyone is welcome to attend. Speaking for me, we need strength from all of our available sources to help us be successful here at MSU." Most attendees politely applauded although some faculty members sat silently. As Jay and his friends left the front of the room, everyone's eyes shifted to Lynda standing by as the emcee.

What should Lynda do and why?

To the Highest Bidder

W. Houston Dougharty
Lewis and Clark College

Lynn is in her first year as a resident director at MacKay State University (MSU), a medium-size, comprehensive campus of 11,000 students in the Rocky Mountains. She is excited to also be serving as advisor to the Service Volunteer Corps (SVC), a group that has garnered much respect and honor through the years and which also has a deep sense of tradition—both as an organization and as a service arm of the campus. Each year the SVC on the MSU campus sponsors a live auction to raise money for a worthy charity in the community. This year the proceeds will go to a local day shelter for teens who are in foster care or having trouble at home.

Lynn's supervisor, Daniel, encouraged Lynn to use this as easy duty for her first year on campus. Daniel said, "SVC tends to have their act together, so you won't have to focus much on them. That should make it easier to concentrate on some other projects that really will require your attention. The faculty member who advised SVC for years before you accepted the role said that he just let the leaders run with it. He said that he basically signed their forms and stayed out of their way."

As a result of this conversation, her own observations of the group, and some challenges she had been having in her hall, Lynn decided to play a laid back, hands-off role as their advisor and was glad that the SVC seemed so comfortably on track without needing much from her.

The SVC president, Yoshiko, is a senior who has held other leadership roles in the organization throughout her first three years on campus. Yoshiko is quite organized and a good motivator. Felipe, the junior SVC vice president, handles many of the details of the organization, including budget and liability issues. The secretary, Bonnie, seems to efficiently maintain accurate records of current SVC activities. So far the SVC projects this year have been as successful as ever. When Lynn asked Yoshiko and Felipe how the plans were coming along for the auction, they told her that the auction was already planned and well advertised. They added, "We also have a surprise twist this year. People will love it!"

When Lynn asked what the twist was, Felipe said, "No way! It's a surprise!"

Lynn was invited to be a guest of honor at the auction, and the leaders said she could bring a guest. While Lynn had not come out to many people on campus, her same-sex partner lived with her on campus, though she didn't work on campus or come to many events. Lynn thought this would be a great time to include her partner in campus life, so she responded that she and a guest would attend.

The auction had a packed house, but Lynn and her partner were ushered to special front row seats right in front of the auctioneer, an off-campus professional who owned a local antiques auction house. As the auction began, Lynn realized that most of the "items" up for bid were actually people—including most of the SVC leaders. Additionally, the auctioneer used coarse language as he offered up a date with each student to the raucous bidders.

"Come on gals, don't you think this hunk could be your perfect man?" he shouted. "Guys, you'll never have the chance to get such a luscious babe at this price again!"

Lynn and her partner were very uncomfortable, but the SVC leaders as well as the large and vocal crowd seemed to be having a great time.

Lynn noticed that the SVC vice president, Felipe, was now up on the auction block and the bidders were in a frenzy. One of the most enthusiastic bidders in the crowd was Travis, the vice president of the Queer Student Alliance. Lynn had gotten to know Travis fairly well in her short time at MacKay. It was immediately evident that the auctioneer had not acknowledged Travis or entered his bids. Travis looked at Lynn silently as the auctioneer's gavel fell and Felipe was "sold" to a young woman. Lynn's partner leaned over and asked if they could leave.

What should Lynn do and why?

Black History Month Collaboration

Karla Carney
Cornell College

Jane, who is 24 years old and received her undergraduate degree two years ago, is in her second year as student activities coordinator at Warden College, a small private liberal arts institution that has a historical affiliation with a major Protestant religious denomination. Jane is responsible for advising the Campus Activities Board and overseeing space reservations in Warden's Student Center. The center's gallery space typically showcases educational displays created by students around theme days, weeks, or months (e.g., Black History Month, Women's History Month). Individual students can request space for the spring semester starting on November 1 on a first-come, first-served basis, and activities sponsored by the Campus Activities Board are given scheduling priority. The rotating gallery exhibits are extremely popular among students, many of whom make it a priority to tour the gallery shortly after new exhibits are installed and visit with exhibit sponsors during opening night receptions. Many student organizations consider their gallery exhibits to be a great asset in recruiting new members.

John, the student chair of the Campus Activities Board (CAB), is also a member of the Black Cultural Organization (BCO) that has often sponsored campuswide programming during Black History Month. Andrea is the President of Sisters 4 Sisters (an organization for women students of color) and is working closely with her group's programming initiatives during Black History Month. The goals of Sisters 4 Sisters and BCO have diverged in recent years, with BCO tending to focus more on social programming for students and Sisters 4 Sisters tending to sponsor activism and diversity educational programming. Additionally, Jane noticed what she characterized as personality conflicts among the organizations' officers growing as the fall semester progressed.

Toward the end of October, John made reservations for CAB's spring events and included a request for the use of the gallery throughout February. At 12:01 a.m. on November 1, Andrea e-mailed a request for the gallery throughout February for Sisters 4 Sisters. After talking with John and Andrea separately, Jane determined that John's reservation for the gallery was for BCO, not CAB, and that both BCO and Sisters 4 Sisters have planned displays honoring the accomplishments of African Americans throughout history in recognition of Black History Month.

At the Student Organization Kick-off Retreat last September, Jane had stressed her goal of collaboration and joint programming and reminded the organization representatives of the proliferation of student clubs and organizations at Warden along with a decrease in student fees that fund student organizations. Jane had many times since then suggested to student groups that they collaborate on specific projects and events, so she suggested to John and Andrea via a joint e-mail that BCO and Sisters 4 Sisters work together on the display or work out a compromise on the space. John's e-mail response was, "Sure, no problem. Andrea and I will talk about it this week."

Andrea did not reply to the e-mail and instead scheduled an appointment to talk with Jane. Andrea arrived for the meeting with the Sisters 4 Sisters advisor, Dr. Greene, who was a highly respected faculty member in Ethnic Studies. During an impassioned discussion, Andrea tearfully remarked, "Why is it that you staff members here assume that all Black people can work together? It's so ridiculous. We don't always have the same agenda."

Dr. Greene agreed with Andrea's position that the groups should not be expected to work together, stating, "These are two separate groups with different priorities. Asking them to combine their programs dilutes the value and the impact of what Sisters 4 Sisters has planned as a meaningful educational experience for all students."

Ultimately, Andrea refused to collaborate with BCO and insisted that Jane decide who has rightful priority over the gallery space for February. Andrea added, "And John was wrong when he tried to sneak in the gallery reservation as CAB president. That was unfair, and he shouldn't be rewarded for doing it."

What should Jane do and why?

Penguin or Prejudice?

W. Houston Dougharty
Lewis and Clark College

Two Rivers College (TRC) is a small, private, liberal arts college in the rural South with approximately 1,500 students. TRC was founded by a conservative Protestant religious denomination, but more recently, TRC is better known for its socially progressive institutional mission, its campus ethos of inclusion and respect, and its highly regarded fine arts academic programs. Because of a number of recent retirements, many TRC faculty members, particularly those in the arts, are younger than other TRC professors. The fine arts faculty members are pleased that TRC has seemed to value their work, some of which is nontraditional and experimental. Additionally, their fine arts courses have become very popular among TRC students.

The busy student union is the center of campus life, and this new, multistory facility contains gallery and performance spaces, student organization offices, administrative offices, a convenience store and food court, student mailboxes, and several meeting rooms. The hub, next to the food court, is a popular spot for the more than 60 recognized clubs and organizations to post notices of upcoming events and other information. Kris, TRC's student activities coordinator (and hub manager), received his master's degree this past May and began work at TRC in July. One of Kris's biggest challenges thus far has been to train his student staff to determine which notices and advertisements are out of compliance with building policy in terms of relevance and appropriateness.

As Kris walked toward his office in the union one afternoon in midfall, he received a harried call on his cell phone from Collette, one of his student managers. She said, "Kris, please come over here as soon as you can! Ashley, Kevin, and Donnell of the Students of Color Alliance are angry about a poster we hung up in the hub this morning. They won't leave until they talk to you."

Kris walked quickly over to the hub and found the three students, all leaders of the Alliance, a well-respected and very active TRC coalition of students of color affinity groups, standing with Collette. Although Kris didn't know them very well, he recognized Ashley and Donnell from the fall student leadership workshop that Kris planned and led, and Kris had helped Kevin with arrangements for some events held earlier this semester in the union. They all were standing near an oversized poster featuring large, hand-painted caricatures of penguins, one wearing a tuxedo and the other a ball gown. The penguin in the ball gown also wore a sash painted with diagonal stripes in rainbow colors. A rectangular, painted frame surrounded the two penguins, and the word "Drag!" was painted at the penguins' feet.

Kris greeted the students and asked, "What's going on?"

Donnell replied, gesturing to the poster, "Look at this! Don't you see? It's obviously blackface."

Ashley and Kevin nodded in agreement while Collette stood by silently, looking puzzled. Kris looked more closely at the poster and realized that the penguin in the gown had a cartoonish face that could be interpreted as derogatory. But he also realized that his staffers might not have made such a connection. He looked again at the sash and the word "Drag!" and suddenly remembered the LGBTQ (Lesbian, Gay, Bisexual, Transgender, Queer) Rainbow Club's annual drag show scheduled for next weekend. He suspected the poster might be an advertisement for the event.

Kris told the Alliance leaders that he would take the posters to his office until he could verify where they were from and what they were advertising. Ashley asked skeptically, "But you do agree that blackface has no place on this campus, right?"

Kris nodded and said, "I do understand that blackface caricatures can be offensive."

As Kris walked upstairs to his office, he ran into a student affairs colleague, Marshall, who advises the Rainbow Club. Marshall stopped Kris and said, "Hey, what are you doing with the drag penguins? The students just put that up this morning."

Kris told Marshall briefly what had occurred. Marshall smiled and said, "Yes, that's just what Professor Timmin told the students to expect, and that they should stick to their guns on this." When he saw Kris's puzzled expression, Marshall invited Kris into his office.

"See," Marshall explained, "the posters are a tease to attract interest in the drag show, but they're also meant to provoke reactions to the images. Three of the Rainbow Club members are currently taking Professor Timmin's studio art class, and he gave them some ideas on how to not only advertise the event but make it an artistic statement. The end result was the drag penguins poster. Apparently, Professor Timmin was really impressed with their project, and the students were so pleased by his support that they've asked him to advise the club. I've enjoyed being their advisor, but this will free up my time for other things. Oh, and here's part two of the drag penguins." Marshall located a piece of paper on his desk and handed it to Kris. "The club members have made a whole stack of these flyers. These will be in students' mailboxes tomorrow, after everyone's had a chance today to see the poster by itself, with just the penguins."

The flyer contained a small image of the poster followed by these words:

These images of the Drag King and Queen penguins are a complex statement of Rainbow symbolism and gender identity. The gay penguin is our mascot. Zoos around the world have observed pairs of same-gender penguins in long, stable relationships. We want to embrace the image of gay relationships in a universal context. Penguins are also considered a cute, friendly animal, and we want an approachable image for the gay community on campus. The next layer of the image is celebrating the people in the Drag Community. When people dress in drag, they enhance and often exaggerate their features to embody their own expressions of gender imagery. The large eyes and lips of the Penguin Drag Queen are meant to represent and celebrate a drag queen's face. Please accept these images as our celebration of gender, and please come to the Rainbow Club's drag show. Next Saturday night, 9 p.m., Union Commons.

As Kris finished reading the flyer, Collette leaned into the doorway of Marshall's office and said, "Kris, the guy who asked to have the penguin poster put up in the hub is here with Professor Timmin. They want to know why the poster was taken down."

What should Kris do and why?

7

Mentoring and Professional Advancement Cases

Supervising and Role Modeling

Lori Patton
Iowa State University

Mona is transitioning from two years of residence life experience at a small college to a new role as coordinator of student activities at Chase College. Chase College is a midsized, private, liberal arts institution with 9,000 students. The student activities office is housed in the student affairs department, and Mona reports to Ryann, the Director of Student Activities. The Student Activities Office has a small staff comprised of the director (Ryann), Mona, Jonas (a second year graduate assistant who's enrolled in the college student personnel (CSP) program at a nearby university), a shared office assistant, and two student workers. Mona is excited about this position and also somewhat nervous, because this will be a new experience at a new institution. When Mona interviewed for the position, she felt particularly proud when Larry, the dean of students and Ryann's direct supervisor, shook her hand and told her warmly, "We really must have solid commitment and leadership in this area. Your background looks strong, and I'm glad you're interested in the position."

The day Mona started at Chase, Larry had stopped by Mona's office to welcome her and tell her to contact him if she needed anything.

Mona hoped that Ryann would be a great mentor and supervisor, something she felt was lacking in her first professional position. During the first few months of the job, things went smoothly, although Ryann often sought Mona's advice on personal issues, sometimes making Mona a little uncomfortable. Despite this, Mona was transitioning well, felt that she had established a good relationship with Ryann, and viewed Ryann as a good mentor and supervisor.

Homecoming at Chase is a traditional event, and one of Chase's largest events, involving the entire campus community. Moreover, it attracts many alumni, parents, and friends of the college. Ryann had already done some initial planning last spring with the five-student Homecoming Planning Committee, but she passed the committee advising role to Mona once Mona joined the staff.

At her first meeting with the planning committee, the students had voiced disagreement with some of the recommendations that Mona made. After this meeting, two committee members had discussed the issues with Ryann. Ryann told the students that she agreed with their ideas, and the students told Mona this at the next planning committee. Mona spoke with Ryann to better understand the situation and added, "I made those recommendations in the interest of the students, whether they realize it or not. I was hoping to get your support on this."

Ryann replied, "Mona, I totally understand your point of view. However, the committee had begun their planning prior to your start date and had developed a lot of ownership of the event. I think it will be easier if we go with what was originally planned. Next year, it will be easier to introduce changes."

Although Mona remained concerned with how Ryann had handled the situation, she accepted the decision and continued her work with the students. However, Mona felt that, in subsequent interactions with the students, Ryann was perceived as the nice one, while Mona had become the mean one.

As Homecoming weekend approached, Ryann, Mona, and Jonas agreed on the logistics for being present at all of the events. However, Ryann called Mona Friday morning to let her know that she would not be able to attend due to unforeseen circumstances. Ryann gave no details, but told Mona that she had arranged for Justin, a residence hall director with two years' experience at Chase and active involvement helping cover campus events including Homecoming, to attend and provide assistance or back-up where needed. Ryann also shared, "I just spoke with Larry as well. He and I are confident that you will do a fantastic job."

The Homecoming events, including the parade, pep rally, and concert, were all successful, and Mona was overjoyed. However, Mona was also frustrated, because at several points during the weekend, she had been approached with questions she could not answer and requests to which she did not have enough information to respond. Justin had helped smooth over many of these situations, and on Sunday, Mona had thanked him and added, "I just wish that Ryann could have been here."

Justin had looked around, rolled his eyes, and said, "Yeah, Ryann just can't seem to get things together in her life, and her staff members usually have paid the price. You're the third new coordinator in four years, and things don't seem to change. I'm kind of surprised that Jonas renewed his graduate assistantship for a second year, but he did tell me last spring that he was really impressed with your interview and was looking forward to working with you. Just between you and me, you and Jonas should keep close tabs on who gets the credit for the Student Activities Office successes."

Early Monday morning as Mona walked to her office, Larry stopped her and said, "Mona, I've heard nothing but great things about Homecoming this year. Good job!"

Mona replied, "Thanks. I'm so glad that the events were successful, and Justin's and Jonas's help over the weekend was just invaluable."

Just prior to her usual Monday morning meeting with Ryann at 9 a.m., Mona checked her e-mail. Several people had sent complimentary emails to her and Ryann about Homecoming and the great work done by the Student Activities Office. Ryann had already replied to many of the e-mails, copying Mona, with a general statement of thanks for their kind words and praise for the Student Activities Office and staff. Mona found herself becoming angry and tried to take some deep breaths to calm herself.

When she walked into Ryann's office a few minutes later, Ryann looked up at her and began to sob. Mona asked if she needed some time to herself, but Ryann motioned for Mona to sit down. Mona reached over to close Ryann's office door. After a moment, Ryann told Mona that she and her partner were having serious problems, and that was why Ryann could not attend the Homecoming events. She continued, "I'm so glad you're here, Mona. You are such a great person, and I can depend on you. I really value your commitment and drive. I wish I could be a better supervisor, but sometimes, I feel like you have it all together and I just don't."

Mona was taken aback and sat quietly as Ryann continued to cry softly.

What should Mona do and why?

Discretionary Change

Ginny Arthur
Iowa State University

Steven is beginning his fifth year as associate director of Residence Life at Amity State University (ASU), a regional public comprehensive institution in Amity City that enrolls 12,000 undergraduate students and 1,200 graduate students in a variety of master's degree programs. Steven works primarily with staff supervision and training in the department. All of the residence hall coordinators (live-in staff members) and one assistant director of Residence Life (who does not live on campus) report to him.

Two days ago, on July 1, Beverly began work as the new director of Residence Life, a position for which Steven also had applied last fall. Steven had hoped to succeed George, the former director. George had encouraged Steven to apply for the position, and Robert, the Vice President for Student Affairs and the person to whom the director reported, told Steven that he would be considered a viable candidate for the position. Steven was one of three finalists, but Beverly was selected for the position, and Steven had made the decision to remain in his current position. ASU's press release announcing Beverly's appointment included a quote from the Vice President for Student Affairs declaring that Beverly brought "a new kind of leadership to the department that will set an outstanding example for us all."

Sometime during George's 19 years as director—no one can quite recall when—a few of ASU's residence hall coordinators were permitted to have same sex partners live with them in their apartments. This permission was not mentioned in the coordinators' contracts or departmental policies, but George allowed partners to live with staff at his discretion. Coordinators agreed to meet the same criteria the institution required of opposite sex partners to be eligible for benefits, and George maintained that this perk helped attract and keep high quality coordinators. Steven also generally supported the policy, and two coordinators currently shared their campus apartments with their same sex partners. The coordinators were open about their committed relationships, which Steven believed had helped educate students and develop a positive diverse community in the residence halls.

Before offices closed for the Independence Day holiday, Beverly asked Steven to meet with her about some prospective changes. After they discussed some pending contract terminations and the internal appeals policies, Beverly told Steven that she had decided to discontinue the practice of allowing coordinators to have same sex partners live with them. When Steven asked why, Beverly said, "This practice isn't consistent with state law, and it's contrary to the values I want to see demonstrated for residents and staff."

Steven replied, "But there's no state law that restricts same sex students from living together in residence halls at state institutions, and we certainly allow that here."

Beverly said, "No state laws and no formal university policies permit this arrangement for employees. This isn't up for discussion, Steven. This has been a discretionary judgment for the director to make, and I'm exercising my discretion as DIRECTOR. I'm counting on you to communicate this to the coordinators in a positive way and effect this change as soon as possible."

What should Steven do and why?

Young, Competent, and Handsome

Salvador Mena
**University of Maryland—College Park and Goucher
College**

Cannon University (CU) is a selective, private research university in the midwestern United States with academic programs that are highly ranked by U.S. News and World Report. Over the last ten years, CU has experienced a cumulative 20% rise in the number of Latino/a undergraduate students, and late last spring, CU's Latino/a students rallied on campus to demand better institutional support. As a result, CU created an office of Latino Student Programs (LSP) staffed by one full-time professional. After a national search, Anthony, who had been serving for the past five years as the assistant director of Multicultural Affairs at a regional, public comprehensive university in the same state, was offered the position. He accepted.

As the new LSP Director, Anthony began meeting with a cross-section of Latino/a student leaders to assess their current experiences on campus and create an agenda for addressing institutional and student concerns (e.g., low retention, lack of Latino/a role models on campus, lack of continuity in programs focusing on the Latino/a experience). Despite Anthony's immediate achievement of an excellent professional and supportive rapport with the Latino/a student community, undergraduate students continuously made reference to his youthful looks. During one student group advising session, a Latina student leader commented, "It's great that CU hired a young and good looking Latino administrator. Everyone else here is old, and they don't understand our issues."

Although Anthony felt uncomfortable, he politely deflected the comment and continued the meeting.

By the end of Anthony's first year, a number of Latino/a student leaders viewed him as an invaluable campus resource, and staff members across campus told Anthony that they had been hearing a lot of positive feedback from students about his accomplishments in his first year. The first year of the LSP office had been a great success, according to data collected from focus groups and a program evaluation survey. The vice president for Student Affairs sent Anthony a congratulatory note acknowledging that Anthony's efforts were making a difference for Latino/a students.

Anthony realized that many people had contributed to his successful first year, including a number of student leaders. Juana, a 21-year-old senior majoring in ethnic studies and president of the Latino Alliance Group (LAG), had been one of those leaders. Juana had regularly sought Anthony's advice and insight on issues pertaining to LAG and related matters. Anthony valued his relationship with Juana, given her status as a respected Latina student leader on campus, and she had been instrumental in helping Anthony connect LSP office initiatives with the broader Latino/a community at Cannon. This spring, LAG was honored as CU's Student Organization of the Year, and Anthony knew that this had been largely because of Juana's leadership and commitment.

Although Juana had not said anything to Anthony, he sensed that Juana may have developed a crush on him given how much time she spent in his office and how nicely she dressed for their weekly meetings. One day last fall, he had overheard some of Juana's friends in the waiting area teasing her and laughing, saying, "Wow, you look really nice today! Why are you all dressed up? You must have a very important meeting! I hope he appreciates how nice you look!"

This had made Anthony uncomfortable, and since that time, he had made sure to leave his office door open during their meetings. Although he had met Juana in the student center for coffee one afternoon, he had scheduled all of their subsequent meetings for his office.

Juana graduated this spring and announced her plans to leave in one month to begin graduate school on the West Coast. The weekend after graduation, Anthony and a colleague from the university went to a local nightclub not usually frequented by students. As Anthony and his friend scanned the dance floor, someone tapped Anthony from behind and asked if he would like to dance; to Anthony's surprise, it was Juana. Anthony accepted. After two songs, Juana and Anthony exited the dance floor. Anthony then looked up to see three rising leaders in LAG glancing over at them and whispering to each other.

What should Anthony do and why?

Reference Calls

Camilla Jones
Kansas State University

Jayme Uden
University of Kansas

Kipp Van Dyke
Kansas State University

As a midlevel professional in student activities, Jamie supervises three full-time, entry-level professionals whose job responsibilities include managing the information desks in the student centers, managing the ticket office for the university union, and organizing the reservations for a number of facilities at Cascade State University (CSU), a large, public comprehensive institution. CSU is well known for its Office of Student Activities, and professional staff members and students are actively involved in professional associations and conferences. Jamie's three staff members also serve as the primary advisors to several campuswide student activity organizations including the Union Activity Council and Campus Student Event Committee.

Taylor, one of Jamie's three staff members, had worked with Jamie for two years, since completing her master's degree. During that time, Jamie had a number of conversations with Taylor about her job performance. Jamie shared with Taylor his concerns, "We must all be willing to come in during evenings or weekends to help the students during stressful times. If we didn't, we'd be demonstrating a poor work ethic, and we wouldn't be showing appropriate support for the students and their efforts. Not all of our most important work happens between 8 and 5 during weekdays."

Taylor had frequently replied, "I do try to make allowances for these times, but it's unreasonable to expect that I can always be there. And what do we demonstrate to students when we drop any other commitments that we've made to come in at the last minute? It is important to me to have time for my own life and my own needs."

Taylor concluded that they have different personalities and work styles, and she accused Jamie of being a perfectionist who micromanaged her work. Although Jamie agreed that he focused on details, he said, "But there are four of us who need to coordinate a lot of details for all these programs and know the current status of a number of complicated projects. When one person isn't on top of things, it causes problems when staff members have to rely on each other for updated information."

As a result of their conversations, Taylor made the decision to start a very limited job search with the idea of returning for a third year if she did not receive an offer. She shared this decision only with some close friends. Taylor had not informed Jamie of her search and did not ask Jamie to serve as a reference. She told a friend, "I don't see a need to bother Jamie with this right now, since my search is so limited. And anyway, I'm not looking for jobs in student activities."

In recent weeks, Jamie had informed his supervisor about his ongoing concerns with the quality of Taylor's work and her seeming reluctance to show improvement. He also contacted two colleagues, Joanna and Tony, who worked in student affairs at other universities, to describe the situation to them anonymously and seek their advice about options and suggestions for more effective supervision. This morning, Jamie received a phone call from Joanna, who asked whether the situation with his staff member had improved. Jamie replied, "Not yet. But I appreciate your listening and offering some suggestions the other day. I think that some of your ideas may help."

Joanna said, "I hope so. But the reason I'm calling you is that a person in student activities at CSU is a finalist for the coordinator of our student leadership program. You're not listed on her reference list, but I don't know anyone on her list. Her name is Taylor. May I ask you a few questions about her?"

What should Jamie do and why?

Treading Water in the Candidate Pool

Joan Claar
Cornell College, retired

As she sent out two more applications in response to the position announcements for Residence Life director and assistant dean of students for Residence Life at two different colleges, Nicole thought again about her job situation. It was late April, and she was finishing her second year as a full-time, live-in hall director at Graham College, a residential liberal arts college in the Midwest with 2,200 students. Prior to her job at Graham, Nicole had completed two years in residence life as a half-time graduate assistant in a high-rise residence hall at a state university during her master's program.

Paul, Nicole's supervisor of the past two years and director of Residence Life at Graham, had assessed her job performance in March of her first year as poor to average, and he told her that she would need to show dramatic improvement within a year. At their March meeting the following year, Paul told Nicole that her performance had improved marginally but did not warrant renewal of her contract for a third year. Paul also advised Nicole to think about entering another career field where her skills might be a better match. "Sales, maybe," he said. Paul's feedback during this meeting was very general, and when Nicole asked for more details, he said only that Nicole was not a "good fit" at Graham and that he was disappointed in her performance.

Nicole was frustrated but not surprised by this interaction with Paul. She thought, "At least he's consistent." What Nicole saw as Paul's largely hands-off supervisory style, lack of specific feedback, and lack of constructive assistance continued to anger her, and Paul's assessment of her career choice had hurt. When asked for more specific information and assistance in making improvements, Paul had put her off and told her to just do her best at the job. She felt that he was not invested in her, particularly when she observed how much time he spent with the other two hall directors.

Nicole also thought her supervisory meetings with Paul were perfunctory and formal, while her colleagues spoke of their meetings with Paul over coffee, their shared jokes, and frequent discussions of weekend plans. Nicole was dedicated to a career working with college students, and her two graduate assistantship supervisors had routinely praised her skills and her potential. When she had contacted them about her current job search, each offered to provide references and contacts and encouraged her to continue to apply selectively for the kinds of higher level, live-out positions in residence life that she had been targeting. They both agreed that Nicole should avoid making a lateral move now if at all possible.

Nicole's phone rang as she returned to her on-campus apartment. The caller identified himself as Chip, the associate dean of students at Thomas College, a liberal arts college similar to Graham in size and location about two hours upstate. Chip said that he was representing the search committee for the director of Residence Life position, which Nicole recalled was a supervisory and programming position that did not require living on campus. Chip noted that the committee was in the process of identifying candidates for an initial round of phone interviews. Nicole thanked Chip for calling, and her gratitude was genuine—Chip's was the first contact from an employer that Nicole had received in response to the six applications she had submitted over the last two months. Chip continued, "Listen, we've had several really good candidates in our final pool withdraw, mainly because they've taken other jobs, and your resume is next in line. But, you've requested that we not contact your current supervisor for a reference without speaking with you. I've known Paul for a long time through the state group of housing directors, so this was kind of a surprise. I want to let you know that we have to be able to contact him before we proceed any further with your candidacy. Are you willing to let us do that?"

What should Nicole do and why?

Search Committee Recommendations

Karla Carney
Cornell College

As a third-year Residential Life area coordinator, Tim represented the Division of Student Affairs on a search committee for the director of Multicultural Affairs at Garrison University, a midsized, private, predominantly White institution in the Midwest. The mission of the institution focuses primarily on undergraduate teaching although Garrison has a few master's degree programs. The director of Multicultural Affairs works with campuswide diversity programs, supervises one graduate assistant who helps with programming, manages the Cultural Center that is located across the athletic fields from the main campus, and supports all multicultural student organizations including the Black Student Union (BSU), Organization for Latino/a Awareness (OLA), the Womyn's Resource Center, and Gay, Lesbian, Bisexual, Transgender (GLBT) Alliance. Over the past six years, Garrison has had three different directors and two interim directors. The final interim director left Garrison five months ago to take a position at a different university—he had been offered the permanent director position at Garrison after a failed search but turned down the offer.

The search committee included the Dr. Janine Johnson, Garrison's dean of students for the past ten years (who supervises the position and chairs the committee); Darrell, a student representing the BSU who is also the opinions editor for the student newspaper; Carla, a student representing OLA; Dr. Daniel Peters, a faculty member from the sociology department; and Tim.

As part of their preliminary tasks, the committee discussed qualifications for the ideal candidate for the position as they reviewed the position announcement. In accordance with affirmative action policy and equal opportunity guidelines, race and gender were not discussed as part of the qualifying characteristics or the ideal characteristics. The committee spent a great deal of time determining appropriate placements and timing for the announcement that would attract the greatest attention from qualified applicants.

Following the phone screening interviews of semifinalists, Tim was very pleased with the quality of the applicant pool and felt the committee had selected three strong candidates for campus visits. During the subsequent search committee meeting, Dr. Johnson disclosed for the first time that one of the three finalists is Caucasian and that she knows this candidate professionally (but does not know the race of the other candidates). She raised the question about whether race is important to the committee given the position and the relative lack of staff diversity on campus. Dr. Johnson suggested that the committee should not invite a Caucasian candidate to campus if it would not consider recommending a Caucasian candidate for the job. The committee decided to invite all three candidates based on the strength of their qualifications, regardless of race or ethnicity. The final candidates were Amy, an African American woman; Erik, an African American man; and Jane, a Caucasian woman. All three had worked in Student Affairs divisions, had different kinds of experience with multicultural programming, and had similar educational backgrounds.

During the campus visits, Tim noted that several perspectives emerged. Amy hadn't seemed to connect well with the students, although her interest in teaching the sociology program's introductory course on race and ethnicity was appealing to Dr. Peters. Jane was knowledgeable and had connected well with most students during her visit, but some staff, faculty, and students were concerned about her ability to relate to students of color because of her race. Erik was personable and related well with African American male students, but had made, in Tim's opinion, borderline inappropriate and stereotypical comments about women, GLBT students and Asian students. Carla, in a private conversation with Tim, expressed her preference for Jane, adding "What kind of role model makes insensitive comments about students from groups he's expected to work with and advocate for?" Tim agreed with Carla that Erik's comments had troubled him as well.

In the search committee meeting following the completion of the interviews, Darrell shared, "The more I think about it, it's just critical for male students of color on campus to have African American male role models. I've written an opinion piece for the newspaper on this issue, too, and it should come out tomorrow. I don't mean that applies to this job necessarily, but Erik would certainly provide us a role model."

When Dr. Johnson asked Carla for her opinion, Carla said, "I guess that's true. A Black man would probably be the best role model for that group."

Tim looked at Carla, waiting to hear the opinion she had expressed to him earlier, but Carla remained silent and did not make eye contact with him.

What should Tim do and why?

Conducting the Search

Sarah B. Westfall
Kalamazoo College

Philip is the director of Residence Life at Hilltop College, a private, selective, residential liberal arts college of 2,000 students. He is finishing his third year in the position and is conducting his first search for an associate director of Residence Life. Although Philip had hired a number of residence area directors during his three years, he had had no central staff vacancies until this year. Phillip's supervisor, a long-serving dean of students who is a tenured faculty member in Hilltop's sociology department, has encouraged Phillip to conduct the search with as much sensitivity to the college's commitment to affirmative action as is reasonable and appropriate.

Midge is finishing her first year as Hilltop's director of affirmative action and reports directly to the president. Midge advised Philip to form a search committee that would represent the broadest possible range of perspectives. She also summarized the mechanics of search committee processes and suggested ways to ensure as much fairness and impartiality in the search process as possible. In previous searches for entry-level residence area director positions, Philip had tried to post his department's position openings in a variety of publications that targeted candidates from traditionally under-represented communities, but he had no luck getting approval to purchase advertisements in less traditional publications until Midge's arrival on campus. He was grateful for Midge's help in increasing the position advertisements' potential reach, and he appreciated her advice on the search overall. Philip also appreciated Midge's emphasis on setting up an open and fair process and letting it run its course.

The search committee screened all applications for the associate director of Residence Life position and identified nine strong candidates for phone interviews. After the phone interviews, Philip and two other members of the committee were out of town for a week, so the process was put on hold until their return.

During Philip's absence, Midge contacted other members of the search committee to ask why the committee had not offered phone interviews to a handful of candidates she identified from the original pool of applicants. Subsequently, Midge also contacted Philip while he was away from campus and queried him about the status of the candidates on her list. Philip responded, "I don't have my search committee notes with me, but I recognize most of the names. Those candidates were not the most competitive based on the criteria for the position."

Midge asked, "How many of the nine people interviewed by phone were candidates of color?"

Philip replied, "Again, I don't have my notes here, but I don't know because the committee members didn't ask the candidates about their racial or ethnic backgrounds, and I don't recall that any of the candidates disclosed that information during the interviews."

Midge then said, "Okay. This candidate named Rex. His background seems relevant and he looks qualified to me as I reviewed his resume and the position announcement. After you get back to campus, the committee needs to offer him a phone interview."

When Philip asked Midge why the committee needed to interview that candidate rather than the others who had not screened positively, she replied, "At least one candidate of color must get a phone interview. All applicants were asked to report their demographic characteristics on cards that they mailed to my office, and it looks like none of the nine candidates you've interviewed were persons of color."

Phillip told Midge that this imperative to interview a candidate of color was never communicated as the search process was being organized. Philip then asked, "Where is this issue addressed in the written affirmative action guidelines?"

Midge acknowledged that this was not an explicit expectation, but insisted that it was the right thing to do. Midge went on, "Besides, this is a reasonable request, and it's consistent with the College's commitment to affirmative action. I'd really hate to do this, but I will shut down the search process if this candidate isn't offered a phone interview."

Philip said that he would contact her again as soon as he returned to campus.

The following week, the search committee held a phone interview with Rex, the candidate identified by Midge. At the end of the interview, when Philip asked Rex if he had any questions for the committee, Rex said, "I guess I'm wondering why you decided to interview me for this job. I thought that my background would make me a real long shot for this position."

What should Philip do and why?

Career Transitions

Ginny Arthur
Iowa State University

Marie, the associate director of residence at Superior University (SU), received a phone call from Emily one day in January. Marie supervised Emily when Emily was a hall director at SU two years ago. Emily is now finishing up her second year as a hall director at Genesis College, a small liberal arts college. Emily told Marie, "I've decided to look for positions in advising or academic support services. Working in the college advising center for the last two years for my collateral assignment has helped me come to the conclusion that these roles are a really good fit for me. I'm a little late on getting things in order, as you might guess—you know how I take on so many things. I'm calling to ask if you're still willing to be a reference for me."

Marie said, "Of course, I'd be willing to be a reference for you. Can we visit some more about the kinds of jobs you're targeting and my being a reference for you?"

Emily replied, "Oh, sure, but I'm sorry, now's not a great time. I'm running late for a meeting. I'll e-mail you a copy of my resume later this week, and I'll send you the announcements of the positions I'm applying for. I have to go now. Thanks so much, Marie. Bye."

As she hung up the phone, Marie thought back to her work with Emily. As a first-year hall director at SU, Emily had been extraordinarily successful with community-building and developing cohesiveness among her resident assistant (RA) staff and residents. However, Emily had struggled with completing routine paperwork and reports and often responded late to administrative requests. Marie had discussed these issues with Emily, who had been sincerely contrite and embarrassed. Emily's administrative performance improved, but she decided to leave SU after one year. With Marie's support, Emily had sought a position at Genesis College, where she hoped to capitalize on her strengths in building relationships and community. During the two years since Emily left SU, she kept in touch periodically with Marie via e-mail and summer postcards and during visits at the annual national campus housing conference they both attended.

One month after Emily's call, Marie received an e-mail from Emily with a number of file attachments that included Emily's resume. In the e-mail, Emily wrote, "Sorry for the delay in sending my resume. Things have been so busy lately; I'm sure they are for you, too. I just found out this morning that I'm a finalist at Mathers Community College for an advising and academic support position, plus a lot of other responsibilities like advising student groups if I want to. I'm really excited about this one!"

Marie opened the attachment titled "MCC" and read the position description carefully. She noted the responsibilities for student advising appointments and also for handling academic appeals, conducting diploma audits, submitting monthly reports, and monitoring students' academic progress for financial aid purposes. The position announcement ended with, "The successful candidate should possess excellent organizational and administrative skills and be capable of simultaneously attending to a number of detailed tasks, mindful of respective deadlines."

Marie paused and thought that she should visit with Emily further about her interest in the position, but her phone rang. The caller said, "This is Dr. Lou Billings from Mathers Community College. I'm calling you about Emily, who has applied for our position in advising and academic support. Have you seen a copy of the position announcement?"

When Marie said she had, he continued, "Good. So you're aware of our need for a person who's able to multitask, manage time carefully, and attend to a number of details in a timely manner. Would you tell me how well suited you think Emily is for this position?"

What should Marie do and why?

Career Advice

Joan Claar
Cornell College, retired

Richard has just started his second year as director of Residence Life and associate dean of students at Russell Goodman College (RGC), a private liberal arts college enrolling 1,200 students located in a small town with 800 residents in the rural Midwest. Prior to becoming director of Residence Life, Richard was a residence hall director at RGC for two years and was promoted to director/associate dean upon the retirement of the person formerly in that position. Richard had a somewhat unsettled first year as director while he and his former colleagues adjusted to their new relationships. The transition was stressful in part because Julia, the assistant director of Residence Life for four years and spouse of Roger, RGC's vice president for academic affairs, had also sought the director/associate dean position. In addition, Richard was still serving as a residence hall director while also serving in the role of director because of a one-year budget shortfall. Having just recently received approval to post the residence hall director position, Richard was eagerly making plans to fill it by spring.

About two weeks after Richard received approval to post the residence hall director position, Julia requested a meeting with Richard. During their meeting, Julia reiterated her earlier disappointment at not becoming director/associate dean but also noted that the level of her disappointment had reinforced her career goal of becoming a senior student affairs administrator. Julia asked, "Richard, what's your advice about the best ways for me to work toward this goal?"

Richard replied, "I think that, with four years as RGC's assistant director of Residence Life and fourteen years prior to that as an elementary teacher and counselor, a primary strategy for you to consider would be diversifying your professional experiences and responsibilities."

Julia nodded in affirmation.

"Perhaps," Richard continued, "you could do this at RGC, but you should also take a look at one of the two other private colleges or the community college that are within a couple hours' driving distance. To supplement your doctorate in educational administration, you may want to take some targeted Ph.D. courses in the higher education program at State University. It's almost three hours away, but at least some courses have flexible formats to accommodate working professionals. I know that feature has been helpful to me over the last two years." Richard concluded, "I want to support you in working toward your goal. What can I do to help?"

Julia replied, "Thank you. Roger and I have given this a lot of thought. I know that one of your priorities is introducing residential learning communities here on campus, and I think that my directing this effort as associate director of Residence Life/associate dean of students would be a great opportunity for students, residence life, the student services office, and for me professionally. I'm well positioned to attract dedicated funding from academic affairs for learning communities, and I'll also be able to diversify my experiences like you suggested. We could hire a part-time person to fill the residence hall director position that's been approved, and the balance could be applied toward this new position for me. Actually, the previous dean of students had promised me a promotion to associate dean once funding became available, and I think that I could help you secure funding now to make all of this a reality. What do you think about this? I'm ready to get started once you give the go-ahead."

What should Richard do and why?

Seeking a Mentor

Ginny Arthur
Iowa State University

As the director of Student Activities and assistant dean of students for the past six years at Millrose University, a large private research institution, Leitha supervises Tomas and Kellie, the two full-time assistant directors of student activities. Leitha hired Tomas and Kellie this past summer. Both are new master's degree graduates beginning their first full-time positions in student affairs, and both are newcomers to the state and to Millrose. Tomas and Kellie began their positions six weeks ago, and each supervises two student activities graduate assistants who are enrolled in the higher education master's degree program at the local state university.

Although the year just started, Leitha had already had lengthy conversations with Kellie about Kellie's graduate assistant (GA), Jeffrey. In Leitha's most recent one-on-one meeting with Kellie, Kellie had expressed her overall satisfaction with her job and the way things were going. Leitha was pleased to hear this, because she had come to respect Kellie as a colleague and valued her skills and professionalism. However, Kellie continued, she was becoming more frustrated with Jeffrey. Specifically, at the first graduate assistant staff meeting run by Kellie and Tomas, Jeffrey distributed copies of a proposal that contained his suggestions for extensive Student Activities policy and procedures revisions and remarked, "I've spent all summer thinking about this and working up the solutions that you see here." Neither Kellie nor Tomas had seen the proposal before, but they agreed that staff should review Jeffrey's document. They placed it on the agenda for their next meeting.

At their meeting two weeks later, it was clear that the other staff members did not regard Jeffrey's concerns as necessary or pressing priorities. However, Jeffrey had continued to press his proposal at the meeting, saying, "But none of you have been here as long as I have. I'm trying to save you some grief by letting you know all these problems that you'll eventually find on your own anyway."

Kellie said that she had tried to be supportive of Jeffrey's initiative and concern but also firm about directing his attention to the remaining agenda items. Since that meeting, Kellie had received three lengthy e-mails from Jeffrey explaining aspects of his positions on the targeted policies and procedures. In all three e-mails, he had expressed his confidence that Kellie would come around.

Kellie also told Leitha that Jeffrey often procrastinated on projects that he wasn't very interested in. In the case of special events that he had coordinated thus far, he had provided their contracted vendors, such as security services and merchandisers, much less advance notice than had been customary. Instead,

Jeffrey seemed most energized when he was talking with her or the other graduate students about his ideas for plans to make changes within the office that would yield greater efficiencies and campus visibility.

Kellie said to Leitha, "I've already spoken with Jeffrey once about the need for him to be more conscientious about making steady progress on all his projects. He listened quietly and then politely told me that I shouldn't worry about his projects, since most of his work wasn't very challenging anyway and he wouldn't have any problems."

At the end of their meeting, Leitha and Kellie had discussed some additional strategies related to supervision and accountability, and Kellie had remarked, "Of course I will continue to try, and I want to keep improving my supervisory and oversight skills. But I can't tell you how frustrating this is for me. It is just so tempting to write him off."

The next day, Leitha was scheduled to meet with Jeffrey, who had requested a meeting with her. Jeffrey opened the meeting by saying, "In so many of our classes, the professors stress the value of mentors and mentoring for our professional development and advancement and for helping us continue to learn and be challenged. And at the Student Affairs division retreat in August, you made the same point about the importance of mentors to support our continued growth. I want to ask if you would consider being my mentor. I need a mentor, because I need opportunities besides my assistantship work to demonstrate my skills and be more appropriately challenged. I know that I'm capable of contributing at a higher level based on my knowledge and experience—even as a graduate assistant. I need to work with someone with more experience who recognizes that and will help me learn more and offer opportunities that will help me grow."

Leitha listened carefully as he talked about his professional needs, remembering her conversations with Kellie. At the conclusion of the meeting, Jeffrey asked Leitha, "So, would you be a mentor for me?"

What should Leitha do and why?

A Quick Wink

Penny A. Pasque
University of Oklahoma

Dean Kennedy
California State University—Monterey Bay

The department of Higher Education and Student Affairs (HESA) at State University (SU), a land-grant institution, has a reputation for creating a cohesive, collaborative environment among faculty members and graduate students. The eight full-time faculty members admit approximately 10 PhD and 25 MA students each fall. A number of well-respected leaders in the student affairs profession have graduated from HESA, including faculty members, senior student affairs administrators, and university presidents.

Every five years, HESA sponsors a welcome home reception for all current and past HESA faculty, staff, and students during SU's homecoming week. Prominent alumni often attend, turning the reception into a who's who event. HESA uses the reception as an opportunity to solicit donations, which have become critical in helping the department achieve its fundraising goals.

Myrna and Jodie are first year HESA doctoral students. Myrna is interested in studying student identity development as it relates to service learning and often utilizes her own identities as a working class, able-bodied, Latina as examples to explain her perspectives in class. Myrna's closest friend and classmate, Jodie, graduated at the top of her master's cohort and her GRE scores were in the top fifth percentile in the country. She identifies as a White, middle class, now legally blind woman (because of a progressive and degenerative eye disease) who was enthusiastic about entering the HESA program because of its strong reputation for academic rigor. Jodie was appointed to work on a research project with Dr. Paige, a prominent faculty member in HESA who joined the faculty four years ago as a new assistant professor and recently learned that he had been awarded a $3.5 million federal research grant, the largest ever received by an individual HESA faculty member. The grant came at a crucial time as federal and state allocations to SU were in decline. Myrna and Jodie were both enrolled in Dr. Paige's introductory course this semester.

Myrna and Jodie were excited to attend the HESA welcome home reception that fall and quickly realized that Dr. Paige's grant was the highlight of the evening. Faculty members and alumni were enthusiastically congratulating him. Myrna and Jodie noted how proud Dr. Paige seemed, and they went to offer their own congratulations. Myrna shook Dr. Paige's hand and congratulated him, and she noticed the pungent smell of liquor as he leaned over, smiled, and thanked her. Myrna asked if he had seen a recent article related to his area of research, and Myrna watched him slowly step in front of Jodie as she was speaking. After acknowledging that he had seen the article as well, Dr. Paige brought his face close to Myrna's and said, smiling, "I'm glad you're following this line of research, too. With this grant, I'm going to be collecting and analyzing all kinds of data, and there's no time like the present to get serious. Why don't you work with me on this grant? Since I have money, I can hire you, and my office at home has a great set up. It would be long hours, often at night. What do you say? If you need to think about it, you can let me know next Monday at class." He smiled again and quickly winked at Myrna before turning to greet an alumnus who had tapped him on the shoulder. When Dr. Paige moved away, Myrna saw that Jodie was looking at her quizzically.

What should Myrna do and why?

References

ACPA: College Student Educators International. (2006). *Statement of ethical principles and standards.* Washington, DC: Author.

Canon, H. J. (1989). Guiding standards and principles. In U. Delworth, G. R. Hanson, & Associates (Eds.), *Student services: A handbook for the profession* (2nd ed., pp. 57–79). San Francisco: Jossey-Bass.

Canon, H. J. (1996). Ethical standards and principles. In S. R. Komives, & D. B. Woodard, Jr. (Eds.), *Student services: A handbook for the profession* (3rd ed., pp. 106–125). San Francisco: Jossey-Bass.

Council for the Advancement of Standards for Student Services/Development Programs. (1986). *CAS Standards and Guidelines for Student Services/Development Programs.* Washington, DC: Author.

Council for the Advancement of Standards in Higher Education. (2006). *CAS Statement of shared ethical principles.* Washington, DC: Author.

Fried, J. (1997a). Changing ethical frameworks for a multicultural world. In J. Fried (Ed.), *Ethics for today's campus: New perspectives on education, student development, and institutional management* (New Directions for Student Services No. 77, pp. 5–22). San Francisco: Jossey-Bass.

Fried, J. (1997b). Editor's notes. In J. Fried (Ed.), *Ethics for today's campus: New perspectives on education, student development, and institutional management* (New Directions for Student Services No. 77, pp. 1–4). San Francisco: Jossey-Bass.

Fried, J. (2003). Ethical standards and principles. In S. R. Komives, D. B. Woodard, Jr., & Associates (Eds.), *Student services: A handbook for the profession* (4th ed., pp. 107–127). San Francisco: Jossey-Bass.

Gilligan, C. (1993). *In a different voice: Psychological theory and women's development.* Cambridge, MA: Harvard University Press.

Guthrie, V. L. (1997). Cognitive foundations of ethical development. In J. Fried (Ed.), Ethics for today's campus: *New perspectives on education, student development, and institutional management* (New Directions for Student Services No. 77, pp. 23-44). San Francisco: Jossey-Bass.

Hoberman, S., & Mailick, S. (1994). Introduction. In S. Hoberman & S. Mailick (Eds.), *Professional education in the United States: Experiential learning, issues, and prospects* (pp. 3–6). Westport, CT: Praeger.

Jaggar, A. M. (1989). Love and knowledge: Emotion in feminist epistemology. In A. M. Jaggar & S. R. Bordo (Eds.), *Gender/body/knowlege: Feminist reconstructions of being and knowing* (pp. 145–171). New Brunswick, NJ: Rutgers University Press.

Janosik, S. M., Creamer, D.G., Hirt, J. B., Winston, R. B., Saunders, S. A., & Cooper, D. L. (2003). *Supervising new professionals in student affairs: A guide for practitioners.* New York: Brunner-Routledge.

Kitchener, K. (1985). Ethical principles and ethical decisions in student affairs. In H. J. Canon & R. D. Brown (Eds.), *Applied ethics in student affairs* (New Directions for Student Services No. 30, pp. 17–30). San Francisco: Jossey-Bass.

Kleinman, S. (1991). Fieldworkers' feelings. In W. Shaffer & R. A. Stebbins (Eds.), *Experiencing fieldwork: An inside view of qualitative research* (pp. 184–195). Newbury Park, CA: Sage.

Knefelkamp, L. L. (1974). *Developmental instruction: Fostering intellectual and personal growth of students.* Unpublished doctoral dissertation, University of Minnesota.

Kohlberg, L., & Hersh, R. H. (1977). Moral development: A review of the theory. *Theory into Practice,* 16(2), 53-59.

May, W. W. (1990). Introduction. In W. W. May (Ed.), *Ethics and higher education* (pp. 1–17). New York: ACE/Macmillan.

Meara, N., Schmidt, L., & Day, J. (1996). Principles and virtues: A foundation for ethical decision, policies, and character. *Counseling Psychologist,* 24, 4–77.

Nash, R. J. (1996). *"Real world" ethics: Frameworks for educators and human services professionals.* New York: Teachers College Press.

Nash, R. J. (2002). *"Real world" ethics: Frameworks for educators and human service professionals (2nd ed.).* New York: Teachers College Press.

National Association of Student Personnel Administrators. (1990). *NASPA standards of professional practice.* Washington, DC: Author.

Rest, J. R. (1986). *Moral development: Advances in theory and research.* New York: Praeger.

Rion, M. (1996). *The responsible manager.* Amherst, MA: Human Resources Press.

Robinson, G. M., & Moulton, J. (1985). *Ethical problems in higher education.* Englewood Cliffs, NJ: Prentice-Hall.

Schön, D. A. (1983). *The reflective practitioner: How professionals think in action.* New York: Basic.

Schön, D. A. (1987). *Educating the reflective practitioner: Toward a new design for teaching and learning in the professions.* San Francisco: Jossey-Bass.

Sundberg, D. C., & Fried, J. (1997). Ethical dialogues on campus. *In Ethics for today's campus: New perspectives on education, student development, and institutional management* (New Directions for Student Services No. 77, pp. 67–79). San Francisco: Jossey-Bass.

Welfel, E. R. (1990). Ethical practices in college student affairs. In D. G. Creamer (Ed.), *College student development: Theory and practice for the 1990s* (pp. 195–216). Alexandria, VA: American College Personnel Association.

Winston, R. B., Jr., & Saunders, S. A. (1991). Ethical professional practice in student affairs. In T. K. Miller, R. B. Winston Jr., & Associates (Eds.), *Administration and leadership in student affairs: Actualizing student development in higher education* (2nd ed., pp. 309-345). Muncie, IN: Accelerated Development.

Young, R. B. (2001). Ethics and professional practice. In R. B. Winston, Jr., D. G. Creamer, T. K. Miller, & Associates (Eds.), *The professional student affairs administrator: Educator, leader, and manager* (pp. 153–178). New York: Brunner Routledge.

Young, R. B. (2003). Philosophies and values guiding the student affairs profession. In S. R. Komives, D. B. Woodard, Jr., & Associates (Eds.), *Student services: A handbook for the profession* (4th ed., pp. 89–106). San Francisco: Jossey-Bass.

Appendices

Appendix A:

ACPA, NASPA, and CAS Professional Ethics Statements

ACPA: College Student Educators International

Statement of Ethical Principles and Standards

PREAMBLE

ACPA – College Student Educators International is an association whose members are dedicated to enhancing the worth, dignity, potential, and uniqueness of each individual within post-secondary educational institutions and, thus, to the service of society. ACPA members are committed to contributing to the comprehensive education of students, protecting human rights, advancing knowledge of student growth and development, and promoting the effectiveness of institutional programs, services, and organizational units. As a means of supporting these commitments, members of ACPA subscribe to the following principles and standards of ethical conduct. Acceptance of membership in ACPA signifies that the member understands the provisions of this statement.

This statement is designed to address issues particularly relevant to college student affairs practice. Persons charged with duties in various functional areas of higher education are also encouraged to consult ethical standards specific to their professional responsibilities.

USE OF THIS STATEMENT

The principal purpose of this statement is to assist student affairs professionals (individuals who are administrators, staff, faculty, and adjunct faculty in the field of student affairs) in regulating their own behavior by sensitizing them to potential ethical problems and by providing standards useful in daily practice. Observance of ethical behavior also benefits fellow professionals and students due to the effect of modeling. Self-regulation is the most effective and preferred means of assuring ethical behavior. If, however, a professional observes conduct by a fellow professional that seems contrary to the provisions of this document, several courses of action are available. Suggestions to assist with addressing ethical concerns are included in the Appendix at the end of this document.

ETHICAL FOUNDATIONS

No statement of ethical standards can anticipate all situations that have ethical implications. When student affairs professionals are presented with dilemmas that are not explicitly addressed herein, a number of perspectives may be used in conjunction with the four standards identified in this document to assist in making decisions and determining appropriate courses of action. These standards are: 1) Professional Responsibility and Competence; 2) Student Learning and Development; 3) Responsibility to the Institution; and 4) Responsibility to Society.

Ethical principles should guide the behaviors of professionals in everyday practice. Principles are assumed to be constant and, therefore, provide consistent guidelines for decision-making. In addition, student affairs professionals should strive to develop the virtues, or habits of behavior, that are characteristic of people in helping professions. Contextual issues must also be taken into account. Such issues include, but are not limited to, culture, temporality (issues bound by time), and phenomenology (individual perspective) and community norms. Because of the complexity of ethical conversation and dialogue, the skill of simultaneously confronting differences in perspective and respecting the rights of persons to hold different perspectives becomes essential. For an extended discussion of these aspects of ethical thinking, see Appendix B.

ETHICAL STANDARDS

Four ethical standards related to primary constituencies with whom student affairs professionals work, colleagues, students, educational institutions, and society – are specified.

1.0 Professional Responsibility and Competence. Student affairs professionals are responsible for promoting and facilitating student learning about students and their world, enhancing the quality and understanding of student life, advocating for student welfare and concerns, and advancing the profession and its ideals. They possess the knowledge, skills, emotional stability, and maturity to discharge responsibilities as administrators, advisors, consultants, counselors, programmers, researchers, and teachers. High levels of professional competence are expected in the performance of their duties and responsibilities. Student affairs professionals are responsible for the consequences of their actions or inaction.

As ACPA members, student affairs professionals will:

1.1 Conduct their professional activities in accordance with sound theoretical principles and adopt a personal value system congruent with the basic tenets of the profession.

1.2 Contribute to the development of the profession (e.g., recruiting students to the profession, serving professional organizations, advocating the use of ethical thinking through educational and professional development activities, improving professional practices, and conducting and reporting research).

1.3 Maintain and enhance professional effectiveness by continually improving skills and acquiring new knowledge.

1.4 Monitor their personal and professional functioning and effectiveness and seek assistance from appropriate professionals as needed.

1.5 Maintain current, accurate knowledge of all regulations related to privacy of student records and electronic transmission of records and update knowledge of privacy legislation on a regular basis.

1.6. Represent their professional credentials, competencies, and limitations accurately and correct any misrepresentations of these qualifications by others.

1.7. Establish fees for professional services after consideration of the ability of the recipient to pay. They will provide some services, including professional development activities for colleagues, for little or no remuneration.

1.8. Adhere to ethical practices in securing positions: [a] represent education and experiences accurately; [b] respond to offers promptly; [c] interview for positions only when serious about accepting an offer; [d] accept only those positions they intend to assume; [e] advise current employer and all institutions at which applications are pending immediately when they sign a contract; [f] inform their employers before leaving a position within a reasonable amount of time as outlined by the institution and/or supervisor; and [g] commit to position upon acceptance.

1.9. Provide an honest, accurate, and respectful reference. If it is not deemed possible to provide a positive reference, contact the "searching employee" to inform them of such. It is not appropriate to provide a positive reference to move an individual beyond a department or institution.

2.0 Student Learning and Development. Student development is an essential purpose of higher education. Support of this process is a major responsibility of the student affairs profession. Development is complex and includes cognitive, physical, moral, social, emotional, career, spiritual, personal, and intellectual dimensions. Professionals must be sensitive to and knowledgeable about the variety of backgrounds, cultures, experiences, abilities, personal characteristics and viewpoints evident in the student population and be able to incorporate appropriate theoretical perspectives to identify learning opportunities and to reduce barriers to development. Multicultural competence is a fundamental element of ethical practice.

As ACPA members, student affairs professionals will:

2.1 Treat students with respect as persons who possess dignity, worth, and the ability to be self-directed.

2.2 Avoid dual relationships with students where one individual serves in multiple roles that create conflicting responsibilities, role confusion, and unclear expectations (e.g., counselor/employer, supervisor/best friend, or faculty/sexual partner) that may involve incompatible roles and conflicting responsibilities.

2.3 Abstain from all forms of harassment, including but not limited to verbal and written communication, physical actions and electronic transmissions.

2.4 Abstain from sexual intimacy with clients or with students for whom they have supervisory, evaluative, or instructional responsibility.

2.5 Inform students of the conditions under which they may receive assistance.

2.6 Inform students of the nature and/or limits of confidentiality. They will share information about the students only in accordance with institutional policies and applicable laws, when given their permission, or when required to prevent personal harm to themselves or others.

2.7 Refer students to appropriate specialists before entering or continuing a helping relationship when the professional's expertise or level of comfort is exceeded. If the referral is declined, professional staff is not obliged to continue the relationship nor should they do so if there is not direct benefit to the student.

2.8 Inform students about the purpose of assessment and research; make explicit the planned use of results prior to assessment requesting participation in either.

2.9 Comply with the institutional guidelines on electronic transmission of information.

2.10 Provide appropriate contextual information to students prior to and following the use of any evaluation procedures to place results in proper perspective with other factors relevant to the assessment process (e.g., socioeconomic, gender, identity, ethnic, cultural, and gender related).

2.11 Discuss with students issues, attitudes, and behaviors that have ethical implications.

2.12 Develop multicultural knowledge, skills, competence, and use appropriate elements of these capacities in their work with students.

2.13 Faculty should inform prospective graduate students of program expectations, predominant theoretical orientations, and skills needed for successful program completion, as well as positions received by recent graduates.

2.14 Assure that required experiences involving self-disclosure are communicated to prospective graduate students. When the preparation program offers experiences that emphasize self-disclosure or other relatively intimate or personal involvement (e.g., group or individual counseling or growth groups), professionals must not have current or anticipated administrative, supervisory, or evaluative authority over participants.

2.15 Provide graduate students with a broad knowledge base consisting of theory, research, and practice.

2.16 Educate graduate students about ethical standards, responsibilities and codes of the profession. Uphold these standards within all preparation programs.

2.17 Assess all relevant competencies and interpersonal functioning of students throughout the preparation program, communicate these assessments to students, and take appropriate corrective actions including dismissal when warranted.

2.18 Assure that field supervisors are qualified to provide supervision to graduate students and are informed of their ethical responsibilities in this role.

2.19 Support professional preparation program efforts by providing assistantships, practical field placements, and consultation to students and faculty.

2.20 Gain approval of research plans involving human subjects from the institutional committee with oversight responsibility prior to the initiation of the study. In the absence of such a committee, they will seek to create procedures to protect the rights and ensure the safety of research participants.

2.21 Conduct and report research studies accurately. Researchers will not engage in fraudulent research nor will they distort or misrepresent their data or deliberately bias their results.

2.22 Cite previous works on a topic when writing or when speaking to professional audiences.

2.23 Comply with laws and standards common in the helping professions related to citation and attribution of information accessed electronically where public domain status may be ambiguous.

2.24 Acknowledge major contributions to research projects and professional writings through joint authorships with the principal contributor listed first. They will acknowledge minor technical or professional contributions in notes or introductory statements.

2.25 Co-authorship should reflect a joint collaboration. When involvement was ancillary it is inappropriate to pressure others for joint authorship listing on publications.

2.26 Share original research data with qualified others upon request.

2.27 Communicate the results of any research judged to be of value to other professionals and not withhold results reflecting unfavorably on specific institutions, programs, services, or prevailing opinion.

2.28 Submit manuscripts for consideration to only one journal at a time. They will not seek to publish previously published or accepted-for-publication materials in other media or publications without first informing all editors and/ or publishers concerned. They will make appropriate references in the text and receive permission to use copyrights.

3.0 Responsibility to the Institution. Institutions of higher education provide the context for student affairs practice. Institutional mission, goals, policies, organizational structure, and culture, combined with individual judgment and professional standards, define and delimit the nature and extent of practice. Student affairs professionals share responsibility with other members of the academic community for fulfilling the institutional mission. Responsibility to promote the development of students and to support the institution's policies and interests require that professionals balance competing demands.

As ACPA members, student affairs professionals will:

3.1 Contribute to their institution by supporting its mission, goals, policies, and abiding by its procedures.

3.2 Seek resolution when they and their institution encounter substantial disagreements concerning professional or personal values. Resolution may require sustained efforts to modify institutional policies and practices or result in voluntary termination of employment.

3.3 Recognize that conflicts among students, colleagues, or the institution should be resolved without diminishing respect for or appropriate obligations to any party involved.

3.4 Assure that information provided about the institution is factual and accurate.

3.5 Inform appropriate officials of conditions that may be disruptive or damaging to their institution.

3.6 Inform supervisors of conditions or practices that may restrict institutional or professional effectiveness.

3.7 Refrain from attitudes or actions that impinge on colleagues' dignity, moral code, privacy, worth, professional functioning, and/or personal growth.

3.8 Abstain from sexual intimacies with colleagues or with staff for whom they have supervisory, evaluative, or instructional responsibility.

3.9 Assure that participation by staff in planned activities that emphasize self-disclosure or other relatively intimate or personal involvement is voluntary and that the leader(s) of such activities do not have administrative, supervisory, or evaluative authority over participants.

3.10 Evaluate job performance of subordinates regularly and recommend appropriate actions to enhance professional development and improve performance.

3.11 Define job responsibilities, decision-making procedures, mutual expectations, accountability procedures, and evaluation criteria with subordinates and supervisors.

3.12 Provide fair and honest assessments and feedback for colleagues' job performance and provide opportunities for professional growth as appropriate.

3.13 Seek evaluations of their job performance and/or services they provide.

3.14 Disseminate information that accurately describes the responsibilities of position vacancies, required qualifications, and the institution.

3.15 Adhere to ethical practices when facilitating or participating in a selection process by [a] representing the department and institution honestly and accurately [b] periodically notify applicants of their status; [c] adhere to established guidelines, protocol, and standards for the selection process; and [d] provide accurate information about the resources available to applicants once employed.

3.16 Provide training to student affairs search and screening committee members.

3.17 Refrain from using their positions to seek unjustified personal gains, sexual favors, unfair advantages, or unearned goods and services not normally accorded in such positions.

3.18 Recognize their fiduciary responsibility to the institution. They will ensure that funds for which they have oversight are expended following established procedures and in ways that optimize value, are accounted for properly, and contribute to the accomplishment of the institution's mission. They also will assure equipment, facilities, personnel, and other resources are used to promote the welfare of the institution and students.

3.19 Restrict their private interests, obligations, and transactions in ways to minimize conflicts of interest or the appearance of conflicts of interest. They will identify their personal views and actions as private citizens from those expressed or undertaken as institutional representatives.

3.20 Evaluate programs, services, and organizational structure regularly and systematically to assure conformity to published standards and guidelines. Evaluations should be conducted using rigorous evaluation methods and principles, and the results should be made available to appropriate institutional personnel.

3.21 Acknowledge contributions by others to program development, program implementation, evaluations, and reports.

3.22 Maintain current knowledge about changes in technology and legislation that are significant for the range of institutional responsibilities in their professional domain (e.g., knowledge of privacy and security issues, use of the Internet, and free speech/hate speech).

4.0 Responsibility to Society. Student affairs professionals, both as citizens and practitioners, have a responsibility to contribute to the improvement of the communities in which they live and work and to act as advocates for social justice for members of those communities. They respect individuality and individual differences. They recognize that our communities are enhanced by social and individual diversity manifested by characteristics such as age, culture, class, ethnicity, gender, ability, gender identity, race, religion, and sexual orientation. Student affairs professionals work to protect human rights and promote respect for human diversity in higher education.

As ACPA members, student affairs professionals will:

4.1 Assist students in becoming productive, ethical, and responsible citizens.

4.2 Demonstrate concern for the welfare of all students and work for constructive change on behalf of students.

4.3 Not discriminate on the basis of age, culture, ethnicity, gender, ability, gender identity, race, class, religion, or sexual orientation. They will actively work to change discriminatory practices.

4.4 Demonstrate regard for social codes and moral expectations of the communities in which they live and work. At the same time, they will be aware of situations in which concepts of social justice may conflict with local moral standards and norms and may choose to point out these conflicts in ways that respect the rights and values of all who are involved. They will recognize that violations of accepted moral and legal standards may involve their clients, students, or colleagues in damaging personal conflicts and may impugn the integrity of the profession, their own reputations, and that of the employing institution.

4.5 Report to the appropriate authority any condition that is likely to harm their clients and/or others.

ACPA Statement's
APPENDIX A

Suggestions for Resolving Ethical Misconduct

USE OF THIS STATEMENT

• Initiate a private conversation. Because unethical conduct often is due to a lack of awareness or understanding of ethical standards as described in the preceding document, a private conversation between the target of inappropriate action(s) and the individual being inappropriate is an important initial line of action. This conference, if pursued in a spirit of collegiality and sincerity, often may resolve the ethical concern and promote future ethical conduct.

• Pursue institutional resources. If a private conference does not resolve the problem institutional resources may be pursued. It is recommended individuals work with mentors, supervisors, faculty, colleagues, or peers to research campus based resources.

• Request consultation from ACPA Ethics Committee. If an individual is unsure whether a particular behavior, activity, or practice falls under the provisions of this statement, the Ethics Committee may be contacted in writing. A detailed written description (omitting data identifying the person(s) involved), describing the potentially unethical behavior, activity, or practice and the circumstances surrounding the situation should be submitted to a member of the ACPA Ethics Committee. Members of the Committee will provide the individual with a summary of opinions regarding the ethical appropriateness of the conduct or practice in question, as well as some suggestions as to what action(s) could be taken. Because these opinions are based on limited information, no specific situation or action will be judged "unethical." Responses rendered by the Committee are advisory only and are not an official statement on behalf of ACPA. Please contact the ACPA Executive Director for more information.

ACPA Statement's
APPENDIX B

ETHICAL FOUNDATIONS OF THIS DOCUMENT

The principles that provide the foundation for this document are:

• Act to benefit others. Service to humanity is the basic tenet underlying student affairs practice. Hence, the student affairs profession exists to: [a] promote cognitive, social, physical, intellectual, and spiritual development of students; [b] bring an institution-wide awareness of the interconnectedness of learning and development throughout the institution in academic, service, and management functions; [c] contribute to the effective functioning of the institution; and [d] provide programs and services consistent with this principle.

• Promote justice. Student affairs professionals are committed to assuring fundamental fairness for all persons within the academic community. The values of impartiality, equity, and reciprocity are basic. When there are greater needs than resources available or when the interests of constituencies conflict, justice requires honest consideration of all claims and requests and equitable (not necessarily equal) distribution of goods and services. A crucial aspect of promoting justice is demonstrating respect for human differences and opposing intolerance of these differences. Important human differences include, but are not limited to, characteristics such as ability, age, class, culture, ethnicity, gender, gender identity, race, religion, or sexual orientation.

• Respect autonomy. Student affairs professionals respect and promote autonomy and privacy. This includes the rights of persons whose cultural traditions elevate the importance of the family over the importance of the individual to make choices based on the desires of their families if they wish. Students' freedom of choice and action are not restricted unless their actions significantly interfere with the welfare of others or the accomplishment of the institution's mission.

• Be faithful. Student affairs professionals make all efforts to be accurate in their presentation of facts, honor agreements, and trustworthy in the performance of their duties.

• Do no harm. Student affairs professionals do not engage in activities that cause either physical or psychological damage to others. In addition to their personal actions, student affairs professionals are especially vigilant to assure that the institutional policies do not: [a] hinder students' opportunities to benefit from the learning experiences available in the environment; [b] threaten individuals' self-worth, dignity, or safety; or [c] discriminate unjustly or illegally. Student affairs professionals are expected to understand that students from non-dominant cultures and groups that differ from the majority may feel harmed by attitudes and processes that are considered harmless by members of the dominant (i.e., majority) group.

Virtues: Habitual behavior. The virtues that student affairs educators should work to develop are based on widely accepted ideas about the characteristics of people in helping professions who are consistently ethical in their choices and behavior. Virtues differ from principles in that they are related to specific contexts and demonstrate personal characteristics that people in that context, in this case the student affairs profession, value. Virtues balance principles in that they are somewhat flexible and reflect the means by which a person acts on values. The four virtues associated with this profession are prudence, integrity, respectfulness, and benevolence.

• Self-regarding virtues. Prudence and integrity are virtues related to the behavior of a person in a particular situation. Prudence signifies thoughtfulness and unwillingness to jump to conclusions. Integrity signifies consistency and wholeness; a lack of dramatic behavioral differences from one situation to another.

• Other-regarding virtues. Respectfulness and benevolence are virtues that describe a person's treatment of others. Respectful persons are prudent—they take time to think about appropriate responses to others in unfamiliar situations. Respectfulness is also connected to benevolence, the consistent habit of taking other people's well-being into consideration.

Context: Finding patterns of meaning and developing ethical perspectives

Because our campuses are comprised of people from all over the world, have official connections with institutions in many countries, and also serve people who are Americans with significant allegiance to non-dominant cultures, it is important to take context into account when addressing ethical concerns. There are three frames of reference that should be considered: culture, temporality, and phenomenology.

• Culture. Every culture has its own ideas about values, virtues, social and family roles, and acceptable behavior. Cultures may be grounded in ethnicity, faith, gender, generation, sexual orientation, physical ability, or geographic area to name a few. Every campus also has a range of cultures based on work status or location as well as a dominant culture of its own. Ethical dilemmas often arise among or between people from different cultures. Ethical decision-making suggests that the values of relevant cultures be examined when dilemmas arise and overt conversations about conflicting values take place, if necessary.

• Temporality. This term suggests that an awareness of time-related issues be present. These include the duration of the problem, the urgency of its resolution, the time of the academic year, the duration of the relationships among the people involved, and the "spirit of the times" or Zeitgeist.

• Phenomenology. All persons have both cultural roots and individual attributes that shape their perspectives. Phenomenology refers to the personal and individual points of view of the persons involved in the situation. Both justice and prudence require that decision-makers do not assume anything about a person's perspective based on cultural background until that perspective is understood in both its individual and its cultural contexts.

References for Additional Information

Fried, J. (2003). Ethical standards and principles. In S. Komives, D. Woodard, & Associates (Eds.), Student services: A handbook for the profession (4th ed., pp. 107–127). San Francisco: Jossey-Bass.

Kitchener, K. (1985). Ethical principles and ethical decisions in student affairs. In H. Canon & R. Brown (Eds.), Applied ethics in student services (New Directions in Student Services No. 30, pp. 17-30). San Francisco: Jossey-Bass.

Meara, N., Schmidt, L., & Day, J. (1996). A foundation for ethical decisions, policies and character. The Counseling Psychologist, 24, 4-77.

NASPA: Student Affairs Administrators in Higher Education

Standards of Professional Practice

NASPA: Student Affairs Administrators in Higher Education is an organization of colleges, universities, agencies, and professional educators whose members are committed to providing services and education that enhance student growth and development. The association seeks to promote student personnel work as a profession which requires personal integrity, belief in the dignity and worth of individuals, respect for individual differences and diversity, a commitment to service, and dedication to the development of individuals and the college community through education. NASPA supports student personnel work by providing opportunities for its members to expand knowledge and skills through professional education and experience. The following standards were endorsed by NASPA at the December 1990 board of directors meeting in Washington, D.C.

1. Professional Services

Members of NASPA fulfill the responsibilities of their position by supporting the educational interests, rights, and welfare of students in accordance with the mission of the employing institution.

2. Agreement with Institutional Mission and Goals

Members who accept employment with an educational institution subscribe to the general mission and goals of the institution.

3. Management of Institutional Resources

Members seek to advance the welfare of the employing institution through accountability for the proper use of institutional funds, personnel, equipment, and other resources. Members inform appropriate officials of conditions which may be potentially disruptive or damaging to the institution's mission, personnel, and property.

4. Employment Relationship

Members honor employment relationships. Members do not commence new duties or obligations at another institution under a new contractual agreement until termination of an existing contract, unless otherwise agreed to by the member and the member's current and new supervisors. Members adhere to professional practices in securing positions and employment relationships.

5. Conflict of Interest

Members recognize their obligation to the employing institution and seek to avoid private interests, obligations, and transactions which are in conflict of interest or give the appearance of impropriety. Members clearly distinguish between statements and actions which represent their own personal views and those which represent their employing institution when important to do so.

6. Legal Authority

Members respect and acknowledge all lawful authority. Members refrain from conduct involving dishonesty, fraud, deceit, and misrepresentation or unlawful discrimination. NASPA recognizes that legal issues are often ambiguous, and members should seek the advice of counsel as appropriate. Members demonstrate concern for the legal, social codes and moral expectations of the communities in which they live and work even when the dictates of one's conscience may require behavior as a private citizen which is not in keeping with these codes/ expectations.

7. Equal Consideration and Treatment of Others

Members execute professional responsibilities with fairness and impartiality and show equal consideration to individuals regardless of status or position. Members respect individuality and promote an appreciation of human diversity in higher education. In keeping with the mission of their respective institution and remaining cognizant of federal, state, and local laws, they do not discriminate on the basis of race, religion, creed, gender, age, national origin, sexual orientation, or physical disability. Members do not engage in or tolerate harassment in any form and should exercise professional judgment in entering into intimate relationships with those for whom they have any supervisory, evaluative, or instructional responsibility.

8. Student Behavior

Members demonstrate and promote responsible behavior and support actions that enhance personal growth and development of students. Members foster conditions designed to ensure a student's acceptance of responsibility for his/her own behavior. Members inform and educate students as to sanctions or constraints on student behavior which may result from violations of law or institutional policies.

9. Integrity of Information and Research

Members ensure that all information conveyed to others is accurate and in appropriate context. In their research and publications, members conduct and report research studies to assure accurate interpretation of findings, and they adhere to accepted professional standards of academic integrity.

10. Confidentiality

Members ensure that confidentiality is maintained with respect to all privileged communications and to educational and professional records considered confidential. They inform all parties of the nature and/or limits of confidentiality. Members share information only in accordance with institutional policies and relevant statutes when given the informed consent or when required to prevent personal harm to themselves or others.

11. Research Involving Human Subjects

Members are aware of and take responsibility for all pertinent ethical principles and institutional requirements when planning any research activity dealing with human subjects. (See Ethical Principles in the Conduct of Research with Human Participants, Washington, D.C.: American Psychological Association, 1982.)

12. Representation of Professional Competence

Members at all times represent accurately their professional credentials, competencies, and limitations and act to correct any misrepresentations of these qualifications by others. Members make proper referrals to appropriate professionals when the member's professional competence does not meet the task or issue in question.

13. Selection and Promotion Practices

Members support nondiscriminatory, fair employment practices by appropriately publicizing staff vacancies, selection criteria, deadlines, and promotion criteria in accordance with the spirit and intent of equal opportunity policies and established legal guidelines and institutional policies.

14. References

Members, when serving as a reference, provide accurate and complete information about candidates, including both relevant strengths and limitations of a professional and personal nature.

15. Job Definitions and Performance Evaluation

Members clearly define with subordinates and supervisors job responsibilities and decision-making procedures, mutual expectations, accountability procedures, and evaluation criteria.

16. Campus Community

Members promote a sense of community among all areas of the campus by working cooperatively with students, faculty, staff, and others outside the institution to address the common goals of student learning and development. Members foster a climate of collegiality and mutual respect in their work relationships.

17. Professional Development

Members have an obligation to continue personal professional growth and to contribute to the development of the profession by enhancing personal knowledge and skills, sharing ideas and information, improving professional practices, conducting and reporting research, and participating in association activities. Members promote and facilitate the professional growth of staff, and they emphasize ethical standards in professional preparation and development programs.

18. Assessment

Members regularly and systematically assess organizational structures, programs, and services to determine whether the developmental goals and needs of students are being met and to assure conformity to published standards and guidelines such as those of the Council for the Advancement of Standards for Student Services/Development Programs (CAS). Members collect data which include responses from students and other significant constituencies and make assessment results available to appropriate institutional officials for the purpose of revising and improving program goals and implementation.

CAS: Council for the Advancement of Standards

CAS Statement of Shared Ethical Principles

The Council for the Advancement of Standards in Higher Education (CAS) has served as a voice for quality assurance and promulgation of standards in higher education for over twenty five years. CAS was established to promote inter-association efforts to address quality assurance, student learning, and professional integrity. It was believed that a single voice would have greater impact on the evaluation and improvement of services and programs than would many voices speaking for special interests by individual practitioners or by single-interest organizations.

CAS includes membership of over 35 active professional associations and has established standards in over 30 functional areas. It has succeeded in providing a platform through which representatives from across higher education can jointly develop and promulgate standards of good practice that are endorsed not just by those working in a particular area, but by representatives of higher education associations.

CAS often cites George Washington, who said, "Let us raise a standard to which the wise and honest can repair." CAS has raised standards; it is now time to focus on the attributes, such as wisdom and honesty, of those professionals who would use the standards. Professionals working to provide services in higher education share more than a commitment to quality assurance and standards of practice. A review of the ethical statements of member associations demonstrates clearly that there are elements of ethical principles and values that are shared across the professions in higher education.

Most of the member associations represented in CAS are guided by ethical codes of professional practice enforced through the prescribed channels of its association. CAS acknowledges and respects the individual codes and standards of ethical conduct of their organizations. From these codes, CAS has created a statement of shared ethical principles that focuses on seven basic principles that form the foundation for CAS member association codes: autonomy, non-malfeasance, beneficence, justice, fidelity, veracity, and affiliation. This statement is not intended to replace or supplant the code of ethics of any professional association; rather, it is intended to articulate those shared ethical principles. It is our hope that by articulating those shared beliefs, CAS can promulgate a better understanding of the professions of those in service to students and higher education.

Principle I—Autonomy

We take responsibility for our actions and both support and empower an individual's and group's freedom of choice.

1. We strive for quality and excellence in the work that we do.

2. We respect one's freedom of choice.

3. We believe that individuals, ourselves and others, are responsible for their own behavior and learning.

4. We promote positive change in individuals and in society through education.

5. We foster an environment where people feel empowered to make decisions.

6. We hold ourselves and others accountable.

7. We study, discuss, investigate, teach, conduct research, and publish freely within the academic community.

8. We engage in continuing education and professional development.

Principle II—Non-Malfeasance

We pledge to do no harm.

1. We collaborate with others for the good of those whom we serve

2. We interact in ways that promote positive outcomes

3. We create environments that are educational and supportive of the growth and development of the whole person

4. We exercise role responsibilities in a manner that respects the rights and property of others without exploiting or abusing power

Principle III – Beneficence

We engage in altruistic attitudes and actions that promote goodness and contribute to the health and welfare of others.

1. We treat others courteously

2. We consider the thoughts and feelings of others

3. We work toward positive and beneficial outcomes

Principle IV—Justice

We actively promote human dignity and endorse equality and fairness for everyone.

1. We treat others with respect and fairness, preserving their dignity, honoring their differences, promoting their welfare

2. We recognize diversity and embrace a cross-cultural approach in support of the worth, dignity, potential, and uniqueness of people within their social and cultural contexts

3. We eliminate barriers that impede student learning and development or discriminate against full participation by all students

4. We extend fundamental fairness to all persons

5. We operate within the framework of laws and policies

6. We respect the rights of individuals and groups to express their opinions

7. We assess students in a valid, open, and fair manner and one consistent with learning objectives

8. We examine the influence of power on the experience of diversity to reduce marginalization and foster community

Principle V—Fidelity

We are faithful to an obligation, trust, or duty.

1. We maintain confidentiality of interactions, student records, and information related to legal and private matters

2. We avoid conflicts of interest or the appearance thereof

3. We honor commitments made within the guidelines of established policies and procedures

4. We demonstrate loyalty and commitment to institutions that employ us

5. We exercise good stewardship of resources

Principle VI—Veracity

We seek and convey the truth in our words and actions.

1. We act with integrity and honesty in all endeavors and interactions

2. We relay information accurately

3. We communicate all relevant facts and information while respecting privacy and confidentiality

Principle VII—Affiliation

We actively promote connected relationships among all people and foster community.

1. We create environments that promote connectivity

2. We promote authenticity, mutual empathy, and engagement within human interactions

When professionals act in accordance with ethical principles, program quality and excellence are enhanced and ultimately students are better served. As professionals providing services in higher education, we are committed to upholding these shared ethical principles, for the benefit of our students, our professions, and higher education.

Some concepts for this code were taken from:

Kitchner, K. (1985). Ethical principles and ethical decisions in student affairs. In H. Canon & R. Brown (Eds.), Applied ethics in student services (New Directions in Student Services No. 30, pp. 17–30). San Francisco: Jossey-Bass.

Note: The individual items within the CAS Statement of Shared Ethical Principles (above) have been assigned numbers in order to facilitate referencing relevant aspects in other sections of this book. In the original CAS Statement, all individual items are formatted using bullets, not numbers. Our use of numbers here for referencing purposes should not be construed as assigning priority order among the individual items. This is neither our intention nor, apparently, the intention of the CAS Statement authors.

Appendix B:
Professional Ethics Continuum Exercise

Created by Mimi Benjamin

This activity is useful in a classroom or training situation to discuss ethical issues. Below are some potentially common, or everyday, ethical situations. For each ethical situation, standards from NASPA, ACPA, and CAS that may be relevant to the situation are referenced as well as some general points to consider. All excerpts from the respective statements are contained in the full statements in Appendix A.

Directions:
All participants should stand against one wall in a room. One end of this wall will be for one extreme position; the other end of the wall is the other extreme position. Two statements representing these extreme positions will be read, and each person will need to determine where on the continuum to place herself or himself. Individuals may place themselves at either extreme or somewhere in the middle.

Ground Rules:
• Understand that the small amount of information provided may be frustrating but may also be representative in terms of the amount of information you may receive in situations about which you will be making initial decisions.
• Be respectful and accepting of where each person chooses to put herself or himself on the continuum.
• Allow people to explain or share their reasoning, but know that everyone is not expected to do that nor is there any need to defend your decision.
• Be prepared to share some thoughts about why you placed yourself where you did on the continuum if you are comfortable.
• Consider the potential consequences of each choice in a professional setting.
• Consider how you might engage or respond to a supervisor or peer who is on the other end of the continuum.

1.	If this were my area, I would do or encourage, safer sex programming.	or	If this were my area, I would not do or encourage, safer sex programming.

General points to consider: Institutional factors and values, personal values and integrity.

Refer to the following statements in Appendix A:
Among the relevant ACPA standards: 3.1, 3.2, 4.2
Among the relevant NASPA standards: 1, 2, 5, 6
Among the relevant CAS standards: Non-Malfeasance [3] Fidelity [4]

Other relevant guidelines, standards, principles, or considerations:

2.   I would have a   or   I would not have a
        consensual sexual   consensual sexual
        relationship with a student.   relationship with a student.
. . . if the student is my age or older?
. . . if the student is a graduate student?
. . . if the student is in a special weekend program or attending part-time?
. . . if the student is also a fellow professional?

General points to consider: Institutional policies, professional reputation, personal values and integrity, exercises of power.

Refer to the statements in Appendix A:
Among the relevant ACPA standards: 2.2, 2.4, 4.4
Among the relevant NASPA standards: 7
Among the relevant CAS standards: Non-Malfeasance [4]

Other relevant guidelines, standards, principles, or considerations:

3.   I would speak up   or   I would not speak up
        if I believed we were   if I believed we were
        doing something stupid.   doing something stupid.
. . . if it was a new initiative?
. . . if it was a long-standing tradition?
. . . if I was clearly the only one with concerns?

General points to consider: Presentation of ideas/beliefs, perceptions of history and tradition, personal values/integrity.

Refer to the statements in Appendix A
Among the relevant ACPA standards: 3.1, 3.6, 3.7
Among the relevant NASPA standards: 1.
Among the relevant CAS standards: Non-Malfeasance [1], Beneficence [1,2], Justice [6]

Other relevant guidelines, standards, principles, or considerations:

4   I would contact/have a   or I would not contact/have a
discussion with a   discussion with a
student's parent if   student's parent if
I were concerned about   I were concerned about
his/her well-being.   his/her well-being.

. . . if he/she were having physical or medical difficulties?
. . . if he/she were in academic difficulty?
. . . if I had a signed release of information?
. . . if the parent emailed or left a phone message for me?

General points to consider: FERPA, confidentiality, respect for privacy or autonomy, care.

Refer to the statements in Appendix A:
Among the relevant ACPA standards: 1.5, 2.1, 2.6, 4.5
Among the relevant NASPA standards: 10
Among the relevant CAS standards: Fidelity [1]

Other relevant guidelines, standards, principles, or considerations:

5.   I would accept a new job in or I would not accept a new job
in the middle of the year if it   the middle of the year if it
were the perfect job, even if   were the perfect job, even if
it meant breaking a contract.   it meant breaking a contract.

General points to consider: Obligations and responsibilities, personal values and integrity, professional reputation.

Refer to the statements in Appendix A:
Among the relevant ACPA standards: 1.8
Among the relevant NASPA standards: 4
Among the relevant CAS standards: Fidelity [3]

Other relevant guidelines, standards, principles, or considerations:

6.   I would consume alcohol with or I would not consume alcohol
an of-age student enrolled   with an of-age student
at my college or university.   enrolled at my college or
                               university

... if the student is my age or older?
... if the student is a graduate student?
... if the student is in a special weekend program or enrolled part-time?
... if the student is also a fellow professional?
... if the student is enrolled at another college or university?

General points to consider: Institutional/departmental expectations, professional reputation, personal values and integrity.

Refer to the statements in Appendix A:
Among the relevant ACPA standards: 2.2, 3.19, 4.4
Among the relevant NASPA standards: 5
Among the relevant CAS standards: Non-Malfeasance [2], Fidelity [2]

Other relevant guidelines, standards, principles, or considerations:

7.   I would share my thoughts   or   I would not share my
     about a colleague's poor job   thoughts about a
                                                    colleague's
     performance with another   poor job performance
     colleague.   with another colleague.
... if I noticed significant changes in his/her work?
... if I noticed significant changes in his/her personality or appearance?
... if the colleague's supervisor asked for my opinion on my colleague's performance?

General points to consider: Professional respect, collegiality, gossip, care, professional development.

Refer to the statements in Appendix A:
Among the relevant ACPA standards: 3.6, 3.7, 3.12
Among the relevant NASPA standards: 16
Among the relevant CAS standards: Autonomy [3], Beneficence [3], Justice [1]

Other relevant guidelines, standards, principles, or considerations:

8.   I would agree to spend a   or   I would not agree to spend a
     major portion of our budget   portion of our budget to
     to repeat a program that had   repeat a program that had
     limited success and low   limited success and low
     attendance.   attendance.

. . . if the program targeted an underrepresented population on campus?
. . . if the program had yielded positive external publicity for the campus?
. . . if the program had been a longstanding campus tradition?

General points to consider: Fiscal responsibility, program evaluation, social justice, outreach.
Refer to the statements in Appendix A:
Among the relevant ACPA standards: 3.18, 3.20, 4.3
Among the relevant NASPA standards: 2, 3, 7, 16
Among the relevant CAS standards: Fidelity [4,5]

Other relevant guidelines, standards, principles, or considerations:

9.   I would share my honest opinion   or   I would not share my
     if I were asked by a supervisor   honest opinion
     if he/she should cut a full-time   if I were asked by a
     he/she should cut a full-   supervisor
      position that I believe had limited   time position
     value.   that I believe had limited
                                               value.
. . . if the person currently in that position had confided that he/she is actively job searching?
. . . if some or all of those responsibilities may be added to my job?
. . . if, because of fiscal issues, a position that I value more might get cut instead?

General points to consider: Confidentiality, fiscal issues, personal values and integrity.

Refer to the statements in Appendix A:
Among the relevant ACPA standards: 3.7
Among the relevant NASPA standards: 3, 7
Among the relevant CAS standards: Fidelity [2,4,5], Veracity [1]

Other relevant guidelines, standards, principles, or considerations:

10.   I would inform my supervisor if I   or   I would not inform my
      had recently begun counseling and   supervisor if I had recently
      taking prescription medication for a   begun counseling and
      mental health–related condition.   taking prescription
                                               medication for a
                                               mental health–related
                                               condition.

General points to consider: Privacy, information disclosure.

Refer to the statements in Appendix A:
Among the relevant ACPA standards: 1.4, 3.6
Among the relevant NASPA standards: 3, 7
Among the relevant CAS standards: Fidelity [1], Veracity [3]

Other relevant guidelines, standards, principles, or considerations:

11. If a former supervisor agreed to   or   If a former supervisor agreed to
     be a reference for me, I would   be a reference for me, I would
     ask a friend to call him or her,   not ask a friend call him or
     her, posing as a potential employer.   posing as a potential employer.
. . . if this person had given me both positive and negative feedback on my work?
. . . if the friend instead offered to make such a call?
. . . if I got a number of initially positive responses to my resume but no offers for interviews?
. . . if the friend called on his/her own initiative and then offered to share what was learned?

General points to consider: Honesty, confidentiality, faithfulness and respect, professional values and integrity.

Refer to the statements in Appendix A:
Among the relevant ACPA standards: 1.9, 3.3, 3.7, 3.13
Among the relevant NASPA standards: 4, 6, 9, 16
Among the relevant CAS standards: Justice [1], Veracity [1,3]

Other relevant guidelines, standards, principles, or considerations:

12. If my supervisor asked me not   or   If my supervisor asked me not
     to document the substandard job   to document the substandard job
     performance of one of my student   performance of one of my student
     staff members (the child of the   staff members (the child of the
     college or university's senior vice   college or university's senior vice
     president), I would comply.   president), I would not comply.

... if the student staff member told me he had accepted another job on campus?
... if my supervisor promised a raise and/or a desirable addition to my job?
... if my supervisor said this was an exceptional situation but he could not disclose details?
. . . if the substandard job performance involved alleged misuse of student funds?
. . . if the substandard job performance involved alleged harassment of other student staff?

General points to consider: Fair treatment, professional values and integrity.

Refer to the statements in Appendix A:
Among the relevant ACPA standards: 3.1, 3.3, 3.6, 3.7, 3.10, 4.4
Among the relevant NASPA standards: 7, 8
Among the relevant CAS standards: Autonomy [6], Justice [4,5], Veracity [1,3]

Other relevant guidelines, standards, principles, or considerations:

Appendix C:
Suggestions for Instructors and Professional Development Facilitators

One of our main goals is for this book to be a useful resource for faculty members teaching in classroom settings and for professionals wishing to facilitate ongoing professional development for student affairs staff members. This appendix provides useful suggestions and resources for enacting the instructor's or facilitator's role and implementing processes that can yield productive discussion of the cases in this book or other ethically relevant situations. Initiating and facilitating discussions on ethics, professional and ethical responsibilities, and ethical decision making can be challenging and possibly threatening for participants. However, such discussions can also model for professionals and emerging professionals the power of consultative processes in situations where they are called upon to make defensible and responsible judgment calls. Furthermore, these experiences encourage professionals' participation in ethical communities that serve not only to assist individuals with resolving specific situations but also reinforce strong commitments to ethics and to ethical decision making (Canon, 1989). Such ethical communities can exist within the profession at large as well as at the levels of student cohort, department or division staff members, or a campus as a whole.

In terms of approaches to facilitate discussions of ethics and ethical decision making, Sundberg and Fried (1997) describe four orientations or roles that enable ongoing dialogue about ethical dilemmas and discussion of multiple and conflicting perspectives. These roles can be adapted to work, classroom, consultative, or professional development settings, and readers are encouraged to consult the original source for more fully developed descriptions of these orientations. The "transformational architect" (Sundberg & Fried, 1997, p. 73) is principally concerned with environmental design and setting a context that invites participation and discussion while monitoring these environments for potential oppression or coercion. We consider this a primary criterion for faculty members who incorporate discussions of ethics and ethical decision making into their courses and for professionals who facilitate professional development for individuals they directly or indirectly supervise.

Because of the nature of their positions, faculty members and supervisors have authority over participating students or professionals that should not be ignored. Faculty members and professionals should consider seriously the inherent ethical problems involved with asking participants to express candidly opinions or personal values that may be tentative, less than fully formed, or unpopular among their peers and others in settings that carry grade or other evaluative consequences. Clearly the potential exists for participants to feel (or be) coerced into discussions, engage in self-censorship that limits their engagement in the experience, or fail to develop skills and dispositions that can support the ethical dimensions of professionalism. Depending on the extent and type of self-disclosure, role-taking, and probing that are planned, full and prior disclosure of the nature of the experience (see, for example, ACPA 2.13, 2.14, and 3.9) should occur. For situations involving significant expectations of self-disclosure, it would be appropriate to engage highly qualified guest facilitators or external consultants for the experiences. In other situations where situational problem solving (of the case situations, for example) takes precedence over processes that evoke or probe personal values or perspectives, creating settings that facilitate participation and reflection while confronting coercive or oppressive aspects are certainly appropriate. In many ways, participant resistance to engagement and discussion can help instructors and facilitators see if larger or more fundamental issues related to mutual respect or trust may need to be addressed before productive discussions related to ethical decision making can occur.

The "interpreter-linguist," "translator," and "reflective practitioner" roles (Sundberg & Fried, 1997, pp. 72-73) focus on communication that leads to problem solving and effective group work. According to Sundberg and Fried, the interpreter-linguist restates and portrays, to the best of his or her acknowledged abilities, the essential detail as well as affective content of the discussion, helping participants better understand and consider various points of view. This role reinforces an insistence on language and clarity to underpin and advance discussions of ethical considerations and dimensions (Nash, 2002). The interpreter-linguist seeks to advance understanding even in the presence of disagreement. The translator assists participants in grasping broader perspectives, particularly in terms of equitable participation, theoretical relevancies, and/or temporality in terms of long-term and short-term considerations. The translator serves clarifying and distributive functions as she or he makes relevant connections and ensures that multiple perspectives are articulated (Sundberg & Fried). Finally, the reflective practitioner, originally described by Schön (1983, 1987), is somewhat more decision-oriented and situates possible resolutions in terms of professional contexts and in light of desired goals and aims. The reflective practitioner is concerned with collaboration, balance, and optimum benefits, and he or she also monitors and audits subsequent developments to ensure fidelity to decisions or terms of compromises (Sundberg & Fried).

Assuming one or more of these roles—and encouraging their development within participants—also facilitates what Young (2001) described as "values pedagogy" for graduate education, which "requires students to be active in developing and defending positions, to be challenged about the justification for their choices, and to confront standards and points of view that counter their personal ones" (p. 169). However, the above descriptions also tend to presume a development status of participants that is reasonably complex and characterized by creating better or worse response strategies rather than uncovering the "right" answers.

In order to reach individuals less well-prepared to engage in discussions, facilitators should be prepared to adapt their approaches. Facilitators should work to clarify multiple perspectives and values as well as help individuals or groups determine reasonable or "best workable" solutions using evidence and sound judgment. For example, following Knefelkamp (1974), they may need to provide higher structure in terms of procedures or steps in analyzing cases and developing solutions. Additionally, facilitators may need to provide greater levels of support and validation as individuals explore and articulate multiple perspectives, values, and opinions. Guthrie's (1997) systematic description of cognitive and moral development theories and their applications to providing challenging and supportive environments for exploration of ethical decision making is also a valuable resource for teachers and facilitators.

Instructors and facilitators can create a productive and open environment for discussion through using a number of strategies, a few of which we have outlined below. These suggestions center on articulating mutual expectations, adherence to appropriate ground rules, and utilizing techniques that invite discussion. These are discussed briefly below.

Articulating Mutual Expectations

Participants in these discussions should know what to expect from the experience, and these expectations should include desired outcomes as well as anticipated processes. The facilitator or instructor should describe his or her own goals for the session. For example, instructors can note that they anticipate the discussions will be exploratory, analytical, and focused disproportionately on solutions to the hypothetical cases and rationales underlying interpretations and choices. They could also point out that a broader outcome could be greater self-knowledge as well as knowledge of a range of other perspectives, some of which may prompt broader reflection or questions. Depending on instructors' or facilitators' assessment of their particular expertise, as well as their assessment of the goals at hand, they should communicate to participants options for follow-up conversations or advice regarding the additional questions raised—particularly if a more general conversation on perspectives and values will not be part of the meeting or program.

To the extent possible, participants should be involved in helping determine expectations, which can then inform ground rules for the session or meeting. Although these expectations may not differ greatly from everyday expectations for classroom or work-related interactions, articulating the expectations and providing examples will bring expectations into sharper focus for everyone. For example, respectful interactions may surface as reasonable for all participants. In this case, either prior to the session or at the start participants can be asked, "What characterizes respect?" "How do I show respect for others?" "What does disrespect look or sound like?" Participants and facilitators can provide answers to these questions that are then recorded, discussed, and displayed. If trust and engagement are expectations, questions like the following may be posed and discussed: "What do I expect from those I trust?" "What helps me to be fully engaged in a discussion or problem-solving process?" The facilitator can refer to these particulars during the subsequent discussion to support and validate the presence of these characteristics or to remind participants of mutual expectations should the tone of the discussion become contrary to the expectations.

Adherence to Appropriate Ground Rules

Ground rules for discussion should proceed, at least in part, from the mutual expectations developed above. Facilitators can also develop ground rules with reference to ethical principles, standards, and virtues themselves, such as rules centered on participants' faithfulness to the process and to each other even in the face of disagreement. Although participants may be invited or asked to join the discussion, participation should not be coerced. Although some mild levels of discomfort or anxiety can be expected, particularly for individuals less comfortable or skilled with thinking out loud or less comfortable with disagreements or challenges, participants should not be actively made uncomfortable through attacks, sarcasm, or being ignored. The facilitator—particularly through enacting the translator (Sundberg & Fried, 1997) role—can guard against tendencies among participants to be heard or to prevail at others' expense.

Ground rules can help prevent negative or nonproductive aspects of discussions, and they can also be used to accentuate common purposes or agreements. For example, ground rules can specify that participants voice agreement with opinions or support for contributions. Participants can then know when their viewpoints are shared but also that their perspectives—regardless of degrees of agreement with others—are valued as contributions. By conducting themselves according to this ground rule, participants can consider and learn from ranges of contributions and recognize the contribution of an unpopular or minority perspective as a sign of trust and commitment. Some examples of ground rules, but certainly not a complete list, appear with the Continuum exercise in Appendix B of this book.

Techniques that Invite and Sustain Discussion

Facilitators should refer to the roles summarized above (Sundberg & Fried, 1997) for the seeds of various techniques for fostering deep discussions about ethical issues. The facilitator's involvement in, for example, interpreting positions, summarizing perspectives, extending or relating additional observations, and speculating on outcomes serves to help focus and integrate the discussion. These periodic inputs can advance and sustain interest in the discussion and remind participants of progress made as well as questions or issues that may remain. This also gives participants a break to listen, think, and take stock.

When questions or new observations are posed, particularly if the new contribution is provocative or unpopular or if the tone of the discussion has become heated, facilitators may wish to ask for a brief silent period. During this time, participants can note in writing their observations, responses or points before anyone speaks. Such a practice can prevent dominance from highly verbal or extroverted individuals and provide time for all participants to gather their thoughts, become aware of affective responses, and focus their subsequent responses.

If participants seem hesitant to share comments with the entire group, or if the group is sufficiently large that quieter participants can escape notice, consider forming (at the outset or at multiple times during the course of the discussion) informal dyads in which participants can share their initial thoughts or perspectives with one other person before reconvening the group for discussion. If this initial sharing does not foster a richer subsequent group discussion, consider asking some of the participants to present or summarize briefly the other person's perspective, which can then be amended or clarified by the originator. It may also be helpful to assign participants (or take volunteers for) various roles such as spokesperson, recorder, clarifier, and progress monitor in order to provide or encourage investment in the discussion as well as the task of addressing the cases. To the extent possible, participants should have opportunities to play a number of the specified roles in order to practice different types of participation. Facilitators should provide feedback not only on the group's proposed solutions but also provide observations and input on the quality and the levels of participation. Highlighting participants' developing skills in listening, consultation, and problem solving can help reinforce the importance of these engaging in these discussions as student affairs professionals.

Discussions should reasonably include questions and probes, and participants may find it helpful to learn examples of questions that invite responses rather than stifle them. For example, asking "Why do you think that way?" although it may be innocently posed, can imply suspicion about a fundamental flaw in one's meaning making or being. The question, "What leads you to the position of _____ (or the perspective of _____)" instead lets a person know that their general point has been conveyed and invites him or her to provide more information and perhaps discover more about his or her own values and commitments in the process of answering. Facilitators should listen carefully to the dialogue to ensure that questions and observations are inviting further discussion and participation.

Participants should also be invited to help invite and sustain discussion. For example, participants or a small sub-group can be asked to restate or summarize a point of view, an angle, or a perspective—particularly one with which she, he, or they disagree. This strategy can also be used as a precursor to that same individual's subsequent offering of an alternate viewpoint or perspective.

Subject Index

Case	Constituents	Issues	Control	Type	Pop	Size	P.
Advising from the Heart and Head	New professional Student and academic affairs staff Students	Diversity Academic and student affairs staff Advising Academic support	Private	U.	PWI	5-10K	33
The Case of the Pressuring Parents	Student and academic affairs staff Student	Advising	Public	U.	PWI	10K +	36
When the Golden Child becomes the Problem Employer	New professional Student affairs staff External publics	Sexism Campus climate	Private	U.	PWI	10K+	38
GPA Calculations	New professional Student and academic affairs staff	Advising Academic and student affairs staff	Public	C.	Tribal	<5K	40
Handpicking Students	New professional External public	External relations Hiring	Public	U.	PWI	10K+	42
Going to Bat for Students	New professional Student and academic affairs staff Students	Advising	Public	CC.	PWI	<5K	43
A Numbers Game	New professional External public Student affairs staff	Public relations Administration External relations	Public	U	HBCU	10K+	45

Case	Constituents	Issues	Control	Type	Pop	Size	P.
Commencement Ethics	Student and academic affairs staff Parents Students	Public relations Legal issues	Public	U.	PWI	10K	66
Building Dedication and Pool Table	New professional Student affairs staff Students Faculty External publics	Residence life External relations	Public	U.	PWI		69
The Partying, On-duty RA	New professional Student affairs staff Students	Alcohol and other drugs Residence life Student conduct Supervision	Public	U	PWI	5-10K	71
Exercise of Religion Among Student Staff	New professional Student affairs staff Students	Residence life Supervision Alcohol and other drugs	Public	U	HBCU	<5K	73
The 21st Birthday Party	New professional Student affairs staff Students	Residence life Supervision Alcohol and other drugs	Public	U.	PWI	10K+	75
Hiring a Diverse Staff	New professional Student affairs staff Students	Residence life Diversity	Public	U.	PWI	<5K	77

Case	Constituents	Issues	Control	Type	Pop	Size	P.
Boys Will Be Boys	New professional Student affairs staff Students Athletics	Residence life Judicial affairs	Public	U	PWI	10K+	91
Random Threat	New professional Student affairs staff Parents Students	Residence life Student conduct Campus safety	Public	C	PWI	5-10K	94
Bending the Rules	Student affairs staff	Residence life Alcohol and other drugs	Private	U	PWI	10K+	96
Judicial Affairs and Star Athletes	New professional Student affairs staff Students Athletics Media	Alcohol and other drugs Student conduct Legal issues		U	PWI	10K+	99
Silent Auction	Student affairs staff Students External publics Donors	Sexism Advising Student activities Campus climate Service learning Fund raising	Private	C	PWI	<5K	102

Case	Constituents	Issues	Control	Type	Pop	Size	P.
Disclosure of Hazing	New professional Student affairs staff Students	Supervision Residence life Hazing Greek life	Public	U	PWI	5-10K	114
Lee and the CEE Party	New professional Student affairs staff Students	Student activities Advising Alcohol and other drugs Legal issues	Public	C	PWI	5-10K	116
Hazing Hits Home	New professional Student affairs staff Students	Greek life Advising Administration Hazing	Public	U	PWI	10K+	118
A Gift for Leadership	Student affairs staff	Student activities Budget Administration Fund raising Greek life	Private	C		<5K	120
Student Activity Funding	New professional Student affairs staff Students	Advising Budget Student activities Student government Diversity	Private	C		<5K	122

Editors' Biographies

Florence A. Hamrick is an associate professor of higher education at Iowa State University. She received her PhD in higher education from Indiana University in 1996, her MA in college student personnel from Ohio State University in 1983, and her BA in English from the University of North Carolina at Chapel Hill in 1981. Prior to joining the ISU faculty, Dr. Hamrick worked in career services at Wichita State University and Sheldon Jackson College. She is a member of ACPA, NASPA, ASHE, and AERA, and she is currently editor of the Journal of College Student Development. Dr. Hamrick coauthored Foundations of Student Affairs Practice (2002) with Drs. Nancy Evans and John Schuh, and she has authored or coauthored 46 articles and book chapters as well as 48 conference presentations and addresses. Her research focuses on nondominant populations; equity, access, and success; and ethics and professionalism. In 2001, Dr. Hamrick was named an Emerging Scholar by ACPA. Dr. Hamrick has served as a visiting scholar at Thammasat University in Bangkok, Thailand.

Mimi Benjamin is the associate director for Faculty Programs in Residential Communities at Cornell University. She formerly served as the assistant to the vice president for student affairs and an adjunct faculty member in the Educational Leadership and Policy Studies Program at Iowa State University. She received her PhD in educational leadership and policy studies from Iowa State University in 2004, her MA in English from Clarion University of Pennsylvania in 1996, her MEd in educational leadership from Ohio University in 1994, and her BS in secondary education (English) from Clarion University of Pennsylvania in 1985. Dr. Benjamin was a coordinator of Residence Life at Iowa State University, the assistant director of Residential Life at Plymouth State College (*now University*), and a hall director at Plymouth State College before joining the Vice President's Office staff. A member of ACPA, ASHE, and NASPA, Dr. Benjamin currently serves on the editorial board for the "Research in Brief" and "On the Campus" sections of the Journal of College Student Development. She was awarded the NASPA Region IV-East Mid-Level Student Affairs Professional Award in 2005 and the national Mid-Level Student Affairs Professional Award from NASPA in 2006. Her research interests include learning communities, student affairs administration, undergraduate student experiences, and ethics.